The Inner Path of Light

Kim Michaels

More to Life Publishing

The Inner

Path of Light

Kim Michaels

More to Life Publishing

The Inner Path of Light

by Kim Michaels.

Copyright © 2003 by Kim Michaels and

More to Life Publishing, www.morepublish.com.

All rights reserved.

No part of this book may be reproduced, translated or transmitted by any means except by written permission from the publisher. A reviewer may quote brief passages in a review.

ISBN-13: 978-0-9632564-8-5
ISBN-10: 0-9632564-8-3

Contents

Introduction 7

PART ONE:
A Universal Approach to Personal Growth 10

DISCOURSE 1:
The Pillars of Personal Progress 10

DISCOURSE 2:
Everything Is Energy 33

DISCOURSE 3:
Overcoming Toxic Energies 46

DISCOURSE 4:
Building Your Energy Defense 68

DISCOURSE 5:
Making Truly Free Choices 92

DISCOURSE 6:
Your Action Plan for Personal Growth 117

PART TWO:
A Spiritual Approach to Personal Growth 143

DISCOURSE 7:
The Fall of Man and Woman   146

DISCOURSE 8:
The Anatomy of Your Inner Being   159

DISCOURSE 9:
Understanding God   186

DISCOURSE 10:
Making Peace with God   202

DISCOURSE 11:
Opposition from Within   217

DISCOURSE 12:
Opposition from Without   232

DISCOURSE 13:
Discovering Your True Identity   244

DISCOURSE 14:
The True Purpose of the Path   256

Introduction

This book is about you, and it is about change. It is about how you can change your inner and outer situation.

The fact that you are reading this book indicates that you are not completely happy and content with your life. Perhaps you are facing a crisis and you are looking for a way out. Perhaps you have realized that one crisis often leads to another and you want to get off that treadmill. Perhaps you have goals in life that always seem to remain just beyond your reach. Perhaps you have a deep inner longing, a sense that there must be more to life than what you are experiencing right now.

Whatever your situation, the essential question becomes, "How do I get from where I am right now to where I really want to be in life?" The purpose of this book is to help you find your personal answer to that question.

Producing change in your life

How do you produce personal change? Imagine that you long for a vacation on a tropical beach. Would you expect that by just thinking about it, you would suddenly find yourself sitting under a palm tree? Or would you take a systematic approach and plan each step of the journey?

Obviously, you are more likely to get to your destination by taking the systematic approach. You might begin by doing a bit of research to determine exactly where you want to go. Then you buy a ticket, pack your bags, drive to the airport and board the plane. By following this systematic approach, you break a long journey into smaller steps. As long as you complete each step, you will make it to your destination.

This book will help you take a systematic approach to changing your life. It will help you approach personal change as a journey that is broken down into a series of smaller steps.

As you begin this systematic journey, your life takes on a new sense of direction and meaning. Instead of being pushed around by what Shakespeare called "the slings and arrows of outrageous fortune," you are now following a systematic path that leads you towards a better life. Instead of fumbling around in the dark, you can begin to see the proverbial light at the end of the tunnel, and one day you emerge from the tunnel (and the tunnel vision) of human limitations.

You can think of this path in terms of self-improvement, self-help, personal transformation, empowerment or spirituality. The name of the path is not important. What matters is the realization that you do not have to be a slave of your present circumstances. You can rise above those circumstances and be who you truly are.

Producing results

In the past, most people never realized that this path existed. As a result, they often experienced life as a treadmill, with no real purpose. In today's world, more and more people discover the path, and they start walking it with great enthusiasm and hope. Unfortunately, many of them do not experience the desired results or they do not get results as quickly as expected. Therefore, some people become discouraged, and they eventually give up on the path. This is unfortunate, because if these people knew how to anchor themselves on the path, the results could be abundant.

If you are reading this book, you have already discovered the path. You know you can change your circumstances, and you realize that you can influence your own destiny. The goal of this book is to give you a set of tools that will empower you to anchor yourself firmly on the true path to personal change. Once you begin to experience that the path really does produce results, you will gradually realize that the path can take you beyond all limitations.

How can you anchor yourself on the path? You can do it through a firm understanding of what one might call "The Pillars of Progress." Discourse 1 will describe these pillars and thereby provide a solid foundation for your personal journey. The rest of part one will give you the tools to overcome the two primary obstacles to personal growth, namely toxic energies and subconscious programming.

Part two will take a more spiritual approach and help you achieve the ultimate goal of personal growth, namely peace of mind. After all, how can you hope to enjoy life if you are not at peace with yourself?

PART ONE:
A Universal Approach to Personal Growth

DISCOURSE 1:
The Pillars of Personal Progress

First pillar: Building right motivation

Many people ignore the need for personal change until they find themselves in the midst of a major crisis. Only then do they start looking for a way to produce change, but so often they are not looking for true change. They are looking for an easy way out, a quick fix to relieve the immediate pain. In most cases this does not produce the desired results, and many people give up with a sense of discouragement or despair. This is unfortunate, because if only people would raise their motivation to a slightly higher level, the results could be abundant.

Right motivation means that you are not simply trying to get away from something bad; you are moving towards something better. You are not trying to escape the pain and discomfort of your immediate situation; you are looking for a permanent change that will take you off the treadmill of going from one crisis to the next. If you want to produce permanent change in your life, it is important to understand one of the most basic principles of the path.

When people are looking for an easy way out, they are usually trapped by the illusion that they can change their world without changing themselves. As we will discover later, everything in life is interconnected, including your inner situation and your outer situation. You might be reading this book because you are hoping to produce very specific changes in your outer situation. This form of motivation is not wrong, but you need to consider how these changes could possibly come about.

Change will only happen if you take an active approach to life.

Second pillar: Taking an active approach to life

So many people desire change, yet they take a passive approach to bringing about that change. Instead of looking for ways to personally bring about change, they look for a magic wand, a philosopher's stone or a quick fix that will magically do it all for them.

Imagine that you need a certain amount of money. What is the best way to accumulate that money? Do you get a job and set aside a certain amount of money from each paycheck? Or do you buy a lottery ticket, sit in front of the TV and wait for the money to appear in one lump sum? Obviously, buying a lottery ticket is taking the passive approach. You might get money by winning the lottery, but the odds are not in your favor. By taking the active approach and systematically saving the money, you might have to wait a little longer for the results, but at least they are guaranteed.

Too many people approach the path with a passive attitude towards personal progress. If change is going to happen in your life, how could it possibly come about? Do you think a stroke of luck will magically transform your life? Do you hope that a knight on a white horse will suddenly ride into your living room and sweep you off your feet? Do you think a divine being will appear and take away all your problems? It may be possible for such things to happen, but the question is: Do you want to sit around and do nothing while waiting for miracles to happen, or are you willing to start with what you have and systematically work towards your goal?

When you take a passive approach, you immediately open yourself to doubt. The miracle you are hoping for might happen, but it might not. You cannot know ahead of time and you cannot bring about the miracle, so your only option is to sit around and wait. When you take a passive approach to life, you paralyze yourself and you give away all power to influence your own destiny. After you buy that lottery ticket, you cannot influence the outcome. The distance between where you are now and where you want to be is a chasm that you cannot cross on your own. Only a force outside yourself can bring you from here to there.

When you take an active approach to life, you have no use for doubt. You define the goal and you plot a viable course towards that goal. You break the journey into small, individual steps. Each step of the journey is easily accomplished with your current abilities. You do not need a magic wand; you need to put one foot in front of the other and keep taking one small, believable step at a time until you reach your goal.

Consider the old saying, "A journey of a thousand miles begins with one step." Now consider what it takes to complete a journey. Completing a journey is not a matter of finding a magic carpet that will transport you to the destination without effort. Completing a journey is a matter of taking one small step at a time, and continuing to do so until you arrive.

If you truly want to see results, adopt an active approach to the path. Ask not what life can do for you; ask what you can do for yourself. Contemplate the statement that life helps those who help themselves.

To fully adopt an active approach to life, you need to find an aspect of your life over which you can gain control. To accomplish this, you need to know the "equation of life."

Third Pillar: Understanding the Equation of Life

Why do so many people fail to produce personal change? Because they allow themselves to remain stuck in the consciousness that they are victims of circumstances beyond their control. When people take this passive approach, they believe the equation of life looks like the following:

> Outer circumstances + other people = your life experience

These people often reason that the only way to change their life experience is to gain control over their outer circumstances and over other people.

Throughout history, many rich and powerful people have sought to gain such control. Many have succeeded to a large degree, only to find that no amount of power and control can produce happiness and peace of mind. You can spend the rest of your life trying to prove that you can do what others have failed to do, or you can take a different approach. You can realize that the above equation is incomplete. In reality, the equation of life looks like this:

> Outer circumstances + other people + your inner circumstance = your life experience

In reality, your life experience depends on three factors, and you have the ability to take control over one of these factors. That factor is, of course, your inner circumstance. Your inner circumstance includes your attitudes and beliefs towards yourself and life plus your knowledge and understanding of yourself and life. The wonderful thing about a mathematical equation is that you can improve the result (what is on the right side of the equal sign), without changing all of the factors of the equation (what is on the left side of the equal sign). By changing just one factor on the left side, you will change the outcome of the equation.

How can you improve your life experience? Even if you do nothing to improve your outer circumstance or the way other people treat you, you can greatly improve your life experience by improving your inner circumstance. Incidentally, you will find it much easier to gain control over your inner circumstance than to control the world and the people around you.

If you are willing to adopt an active approach to self-help, you can easily get started. You can begin by realizing and accepting this simple, but fundamental principle: the key to improving your outer circumstance is to begin by improving your inner circumstance. You cannot change your world without changing yourself. In reality, changing your inner circumstance can have a dramatic effect on your outer circumstances, and later we will consider why.

Fourth pillar: Understanding how your inner circumstance affects your life experience

If you are willing to accept the value of changing yourself, you can systematically improve your life experience. You simply need to increase your understanding of what is going on in your own mind, or psyche. Let us try to illustrate why this is important.

Imagine you are sitting in a park and watching people around you. This situation has three elements. You have the scenery outside of you, an image of that scenery which is projected inside your mind, and the instrument through which you are observing the scenery (your eyes). Under normal circumstances, your eyes are showing you an image of the actual scenery. However, you know that certain factors can influence or distort your vision. If you put on a pair of yellow glasses, your eyes will pass on a distorted image and the sky will now appear to be green. If you do not normally wear yellow glasses, your mind will not necessarily accept the image that is projected by your eyes. Although you experience the sky as green, you know it is really blue. However, what if you had been wearing yellow glasses all of your life and had never seen the sky without the glasses? You would no doubt believe that the sky really is green.

Your life experience is also determined by three factors. You have the outer circumstances, your perception of those circumstances, and how you decide to let those circumstances affect you. You may not be able to change certain outer circumstances, but you can change how you look at those circumstances and how you allow them to affect you.

As an example, imagine a boy whose father often gets mad and yells at him. The boy looks at the situation with the eyes of a child and thinks he is responsible for making his father angry. The boy also responds to the situation as a child and reasons that his only option is to submit to the verbal abuse. Over the years, the boy builds a habit that determines how he looks at and responds to similar situations. The habit resides below the level of conscious awareness, in what psychologists call the subconscious or unconscious mind. The problem is that habits formed in childhood affect people into adulthood. Therefore, the man now responds to verbal abuse with the emotional maturity of a child.

You can improve your inner circumstance by bringing such subconscious habits into conscious awareness and replacing them with more mature habits. In the above example, the man might realize that he was not responsible for his father's anger. The anger was caused by other factors, such as an outer problem or his father's emotional immaturity. The man might reason that he does not have to submit to verbal abuse. Therefore, he can begin to find more constructive responses that will improve his life experience.

Different people react very differently to the same set of circumstances. You can find people who have experienced great adversity, yet they are genuinely happy and at peace with themselves. You can also find people who have had everything served on a silver platter, yet nothing is ever good enough to make them happy. How can we explain these differences? The only answer is that your happiness is not determined by your outer circumstances. After all, happiness is an inner condition; it is a state of mind. Happiness is not a product of your outer circumstances; it is a product of how you experience those outer circumstances.

Imagine you were equipped with a pair of clear glasses when you were born. In your childhood innocence, nothing distorted your vision of the world, and therefore you experienced the childlike bliss that many adults envy. As you grew up, your outer circumstances caused dirt to cling to your glasses, and your view of the world became obscured and distorted. Your present life experience is deeply influenced by the amount of dirt that clings to your glasses. If you want to improve your life experience, you need to clear the dirt from the lenses through which you see yourself and life.

In today's world, many people have achieved great material wealth, success and recognition. Yet because they have not understood the necessity of improving their inner circumstance, their life experience has not really changed. They are still dissatisfied with themselves and with life, and they constantly feel that something is missing. How can you find what is missing in your life?

If you can accept the value of changing the way you look at yourself and life, you will quickly find that your life will take a new turn. Instead of constantly running into closed doors, you will find that new opportunities open up around every corner. Instead of feeling like you are stuck in the mud and getting nowhere, you will feel that you are constantly moving forward. As you build momentum on this forward path, you will gradually begin to believe that the only limits to your personal progress are the limits which you set up in your own mind.

How do you remove the barriers inside your own mind? You can start by seeking right understanding.

Fifth pillar: Get understanding!

Why should you seek right understanding? Because right understanding is the key to progress both on an individual level and for humankind as a whole. Throughout history, people have been wondering why they do what they don't want to do and why it seems so difficult to do what they know is right. In fact, this question could be considered one of the greater mysteries of human existence.

In reality, the answer to this mystery is simple. If people had a deeper understanding, they would naturally do what is in their own best interest. Normal people do not do something that hurts themselves. When people don't do what is best, they don't fully understand what is enlightened self-interest. Because there is a difference between outer knowledge and inner understanding, you can know something in your outer mind without having internalized or absorbed that knowledge.

To build bridges, engineers use a set of scientific laws and mathematical formulas. Let us imagine that we teach the science of bridge building to a group of students. Some of the students gain an outer, or intellectual, knowledge of the appropriate laws and formulas. This knowledge enables them to construct a bridge that is based on existing designs. Some of the students go beyond a mere intellectual knowledge and they acquire a deeper understanding of the principles behind the laws of bridge building. These students can use their understanding to go beyond existing designs and thereby take the science of bridge building to an entirely new level. These students have internalized the knowledge so that it has become a part of their consciousness.

If you truly want to know better, it is essential to seek a deeper understanding of yourself and life and to realize that this can only come from inside yourself. Imagine you have a statement that you know contains truth. You give this statement to a dozen people and ask them to explain it. If you could look into these people's minds, you would realize that none of them have exactly the same understanding of the statement. The reason is that words have different meanings to different people. If you want to fully understand a certain idea, you cannot simply read about that idea. For example, you have no guarantee that the words used in this book will give you a true, inner understanding of a particular idea. However, you can get such an understanding from inside your own mind, because your mind will use words and images that have a special meaning to you. Shortly, we will look at how you can develop this inner approach to knowledge. For now, let us consider why you need to get understanding from inside yourself.

Sixth pillar: Resolving your inner conflicts

When you receive understanding from inside yourself, you are not merely understanding an idea; you are experiencing the validity of that idea. This inner experience has been called by many names. In ancient Greece, people called it a eureka experience. Today, people talk about intuitive experiences, aha experiences or breakthrough experiences. Some people even talk about mystical or spiritual experiences. The name is not important; what matters is that the experience has the potential to resolve your inner conflicts.

In today's world, everyone knows that smoking is dangerous to health, yet millions of people continue to smoke. Many people find it extremely difficult to quit smoking, and one reason (on top of the physical addiction) is that they are trying to accomplish this without first resolving the warring in their members.

People often decide to stop smoking because they have acquired the intellectual understanding that smoking destroys their health. Unfortunately, the outer knowledge acquired through the intellect has very little power over emotions. People often start smoking to fulfill an emotional desire. As long as that desire is intact, it will work against their resolve to stop. Many people find that the emotional desire to smoke is so strong that it overpowers their intellect and their willpower. Some people are able to overpower their emotional desire by force of will, and they manage to quit smoking. Yet this victory often comes at a price. As long as the emotional desire remains unresolved, people still have a craving to smoke and they might have to fight this craving for the rest of their lives.

The key to breaking any type of negative habit is to resolve your inner conflict about the matter. You can do this only through an inner experience that comes from a part of your consciousness that is beyond both intellect and emotions. We will later take a much closer look at this part of your mind, but for now let us recognize that the way to resolve your inner conflict is to gain right understanding. This understanding can only come through a direct inner experience. As our next step, let us consider how to get such inner experiences.

Seventh pillar: An open mind is the key to progress

We have seen that the key to doing better is to know better. What is the key to knowing better?

Many people look at their past and realize that if only they had known better, they could have done so much better. As soon as they attain right understanding, it becomes much easier for them to solve any problem. Yet when they find themselves in the midst of a crisis, people often fail to see the solution that is so obvious later. The one thing that prevents people from seeing the right solution is, quite simply, a closed mind.

The present generation has discovered solutions to numerous problems that former generations found impossible to solve. In every case, the solution was brought forth because at least one individual was willing to open his or her mind to a new understanding of the problem. When the correct understanding was developed, the solution became obvious. It seems reasonable to assume that every problem has a solution. The key to finding that solution is to increase your understanding of the problem.

How can you find a new understanding of yourself and of life? The answer is so simple, yet throughout history millions of people have refused to accept it. To find a new understanding of any aspect of life, you must look beyond your existing knowledge and beliefs.

The Pillars of Personal Progress

Let us assume that you are facing a problem and realize that the key to solving the problem is to find a deeper understanding. Where can you possibly find this understanding? Is it likely that you can find this new understanding within the framework of your existing knowledge and beliefs? Obviously not, for if the understanding existed inside that framework, you would have found it and solved the problem. The very fact that you cannot solve the problem demonstrates that the understanding you need cannot be found within the context of your present knowledge and beliefs.

This line of reasoning is basic logic, yet so many people cling to their existing knowledge and beliefs and refuse to open their minds to any idea that goes beyond the framework in which they feel comfortable. More than five hundred years ago, people in Europe believed the Earth was flat. Today, most people know the Earth is round, yet this fact was not obvious in medieval times. The explanation is that the people of that time had accepted a belief system stating that the Earth was flat. To consider that the Earth might be round, people had to think outside of the box of their present belief system. Because they were not willing to do that, people kept believing the Earth was flat.

If you want to do better, begin by getting to know better. If you want to know better, look for a deeper understanding of yourself and your situation. To find such an understanding, look beyond the framework of your current knowledge and beliefs.

If you are serious about making progress on the path, it is important to open your mind to a new and deeper understanding of certain aspects of life. If you cling to comfortable beliefs, this understanding may pass you by, and you will remain stuck in your present circumstances. Many people remain stuck for an entire lifetime, and the only reason is that they refuse to open the doors of their minds and allow the light of a new understanding to dispel the stuffy air of a long, dark winter.

This does not mean that you have to abandon your existing belief system. You do not need to turn your life upside down and throw yourself into an identity crisis. You just need to open your mind to an understanding that is a little bit beyond your existing knowledge and beliefs. Then keep the doors of your mind open and allow a higher part of your mind to gradually give you a new view of yourself and of your life.

If you feel somewhat apprehensive about new ideas, it might help to consider that certain things are mutually exclusive. Consider the old saying, "You can't have your cake and eat it too!" Likewise, you cannot make progress on the path and maintain your comfortability. To advance on the path you need to gain a new understanding, and you cannot gain a new understanding by clinging to your existing knowledge and beliefs. You need to choose between comfortability and growth because you cannot have both. Choose life! Choose a higher understanding of life!

Eighth pillar: Adopting the inner approach to knowledge

The first seven pillars all point in the same direction, and they emphasize the importance of finding and unlocking something inside yourself:

- Develop right motivation, which can only come from inside yourself.

- Take an active approach to the path by taking command over your inner circumstance.

The Pillars of Personal Progress

- Use the equation of life to focus on your inner situation rather than your outer situation.

- Accept that your life experience is a product of your inner circumstance.

- Develop right understanding, which can only come from inside yourself.

- Seek resolution to your inner conflicts through a direct, inner experience.

- Open your mind to new ideas coming from inside yourself.

When you face a personal problem, you probably tend to focus your attention on the outer aspects of the situation, seeking a solution from outside yourself. But when you are in the midst of a crisis, the emotional stress of the situation forms a wall, or bubble, around your mind. This stress bubble prevents you from solving the problem because it causes you to close your mind to a deeper understanding of the situation. The reason you may find it easy to solve other people's problems is that you are not inside their stress bubble. Therefore, your mind stays clear and the solution is obvious. But while you are under stress, you are inside your own stress bubble and you often fail to see a solution that is obvious later.

The logical conclusion is that you need to reach beyond your present understanding, your present level of consciousness, your present stress bubble. The place to look for this deeper understanding is inside yourself. Let us perform a thought experiment that might explain why this is so important.

Cutting the Gordian knot

Imagine that we enter a time machine, turn the dial back to the time of 800 B.C. and set the destination to Asia Minor, which is somewhere in Turkey. When all the whirring and buzzing stops, we open the door and step out of the machine. We find ourselves in the middle of a city which is, or was, the capital of a province called Phrygia. The entire population is lined up along both sides of Main Street to witness the inauguration ceremony of a new king by the name of Gordius. Gordius was born as a humble peasant, but through the intervention of an oracle, he was elected as the new king of Phrygia. Suddenly, we hear a great roar from the crowd, and Gordius rides through the city gate on a magnificent chariot.

Because Gordius was elected by intervention from above, he decides to pay a special tribute to the gods. He places his chariot in a temple and dedicates it to the god Zeus. To ensure that no mortal can use the chariot, Gordius takes several ropes and he ties the yoke and the axle tree together with an intricate knot that hides the ends of the ropes. Shortly afterwards an oracle comes by, and when she sees the chariot she falls into a trance and utters the prophecy, "He who can undo the Gordian knot will become ruler over all of Asia." Soon, the most ambitious of men begin to flock to the temple. They attempt to untie the knot, but none are successful.

Finally, in the year 334 B. C. the young king of Macedonia, Alexander III, comes by and decides to give it a try. He takes a close look at the knot, scratches his beard, exclaims, "Eureka" (Greek for "aha" or "I see it"), draws his sword and cuts the knot in two with a single stroke. After this, he conquers all of Asia, for which he becomes known as Alexander the Great.

Some people believe that Alexander cheated, but in reality he simply understood the prophecy. The oracle used the word "undo" instead of the word "untie." Alexander realized the difference, so instead of trying to solve the problem the same way it was created, he found the only practical solution. Today the expression "cutting the Gordian knot" refers to solving a problem by taking bold measures. Most people see this as an old story that doesn't apply to everyday problems. But in reality the story of the Gordian knot illustrates a universal principle that can be applied to any problem. The principle we can extract from the story is: To solve a problem, you must free your mind from the state of consciousness that created the problem!

This simple statement is the foundation for any successful approach to self-improvement. The problem with the Gordian knot was not the knot itself but the way people looked at it. The knot was created by tying the ropes together, and people thought the only way to "undo" it was to untie the ropes. Because people had become influenced by the same state of consciousness that created the problem, they thought that the only solution was to reverse the process that created the knot.

This story illustrates how perception can create a mental and emotional wall around the mind, and it can be difficult to see beyond it. As long as you look at the situation from inside this wall, you inevitably become enveloped in the state of consciousness that created the problem, even if you did not personally create the problem. Because of this, you cannot see the solution and you feel stuck. After a while, you might begin to believe that you have no way out of the situation, but this is only an illusion created by your lack of vision.

This points us to another foundational principle of self-help: No matter what problem you might be facing, the way you look at the problem is always part of the problem. One might say that what is blocking the solution is not the actual problem but your perception of the problem. Therefore, the first step towards solving the problem is to change the way you look at the situation. This does not mean that changing your state of mind will automatically solve all of your problems. However, changing the way you look at a problem is the first and most essential step towards resolving the situation.

You already have what it takes

How can you reach beyond your present level of consciousness to find a deeper understanding? Fortunately, you already have the ability to do this, and you are using this ability every day. Most people call it intuition.

In recent decades, some psychologists have realized that the human mind has many levels, or elements. Some psychologists speculate that one of these elements is what is called the higher mind, or superego. Although scientists do not fully understand the higher mind, some psychologists see it as the seat of the more positive aspects of human nature. The higher mind is also the seat of your intuitive faculties. As scientists begin to study the higher mind, people might realize that whereas space is considered the final frontier, consciousness is the ultimate frontier.

Intuition can be described as inner knowing. It is a faculty that is beyond the intellect and the emotions, and therefore it can often resolve the conflict between them. Many people find it difficult to break a negative habit because they have a conflict between their intellect and their emotions. Both intellect and emotions are relative faculties. The emotions will pull you towards doing what feels good at the moment with no regard for what is right or what is in your long-term interest. Your intellect can argue for or against a topic without finding a final answer. Therefore, as long as you are pulled in opposite directions by your intellect and your emotions,

The Pillars of Personal Progress

you cannot see beyond your present circumstances. You cannot find long-term solutions to your problems and you often choose a temporary "solution" that only creates more problems.

Your intuition enables you to reach beyond the stress bubble created by intellect and emotions. Through intuition you can find answers to life's questions. You might not be able to give an intellectual explanation for such answers, but you nevertheless know that this is the right thing to do.

Let us look at this from a different perspective. Throughout history, human beings have been striving for greater and greater freedom. What does it mean to be truly free as an individual? We have seen that the key to doing better is to find answers to life's questions. Can you be truly free if you get all of your answers from a source outside yourself? Would it not be wiser to find a way to get your personal answers from a source inside yourself? Could this be the key to true personal independence and freedom?

We will later take a much closer look at your mind, including the higher mind. For now, let us recognize that you have intuition and that you are already using it. If you were not using your intuition, why would you have started reading this book? You probably started reading because your intuition told you that this book has something of value, something you need to understand.

Perhaps you are already well aware of your intuitive faculties and feel comfortable using them. If so, you can use your intuition to gain a deeper understanding of the ideas that will be presented in the following discourses.

Perhaps you think that this talk about inner knowledge sounds abstract and vague. If so, do not despair. If you apply the technique described on the following pages, you will gradually become more comfortable with your intuitive faculties.

How to get maximum results from reading this book

These discourses are not an attempt to define a new doctrine that will compete with the many existing doctrines found in this world. They are not meant to tell you what to believe, what to do or how to live your personal life. The purpose of these discourses is to help you develop a personal approach that allows you to get valid answers from a source inside yourself.

If you want to gain the maximum benefit from reading this book, take the inner approach to knowledge and apply it to the ideas you read. Because this book is meant to enhance your inner understanding, you need to look beyond the words. Use the book as a stepping stone, as a tool for achieving an inner, intuitive experience.

As you read this book, you may come upon ideas that are new to you, that you do not understand or that seem to go beyond your existing knowledge and beliefs. Instead of simply accepting or rejecting such ideas, you might put them to the test by applying the inner approach to knowledge. Use the technique described at the end of this section to determine whether an idea has value to you. If you will engage in this process, you will develop a unique personal understanding that will allow you to internalize the knowledge in this book. In fact, you may attain an understanding that goes beyond what is in the book.

Applying the inner approach to knowledge

Because you are reading a book on self-help, you have probably already adopted the inner approach, and you are using your intuition to some degree. You can now start using your intuition in a more conscious and systematic manner. If the

The Pillars of Personal Progress

inner approach seems new or abstract to you, start by using the following steps:

- Saturate your outer mind with the idea you are trying to understand. Study the idea until you build what is called "creative tension."

- After the creative tension reaches a certain intensity, let go of the idea. Simply relax your mind and release the idea or problem.

- After you let go, keep part of your attention focused within, and listen for an answer.

To use intuition successfully, you need to apply all three elements, and for many people this can take some practice. When faced with a difficult question, many people find it easy to build tension, but they often produce stress rather than creative tension.

Many people find it difficult to let go of the question after the creative, or not so creative, tension has been achieved. However, letting go is the most important part of the process, and the reason is simple. When you build creative tension, you saturate your mind with the question until the answer has no room to enter. To receive the answer, you need to let go of the question and allow your outer mind to become still so that the answer, which already exists in your higher mind, can surface in your conscious awareness. As long as you maintain the tension, the answer has no room to surface.

The key to better intuition is to consciously apply all three steps. You start by letting your higher mind know about the idea that you want to understand. You build intensity to make sure that the question reaches your higher mind. Then, you let go of the question with your outer mind so that your higher mind can formulate the answer. Finally, you listen for an answer coming from that higher mind. The steps are simple: think, let go and listen.

A step-by-step approach

In the beginning, you might benefit from a step-by-step approach. As you encounter a new idea, in this book or elsewhere, do the following:

1. Stop your outer mind from making a judgment about the idea. The intellect is always ready to judge everything and everybody. If a judgment has already been made, overrule it with your conscious mind. Make the decision that you will not accept the judgment, but you will seek an answer from your higher mind. Neutralize the judgmental part of your mind by contemplating how an open mind is the key to progress.

2. Decide to take an open-minded look at the idea. Apply a technique used by many scientists and ask yourself, "If this idea was true, could it possibly explain something that my present knowledge and beliefs cannot explain?" You are not trying to determine if the idea is true, you are considering the explanatory power of the idea.

3. Decide to consider the idea from several angles. Focus on the idea until you feel that you have reached a certain intensity of concentration.

4. When you feel that you have established creative tension, let go of the idea and send it to your higher mind.

5. Focus your attention at the center of your chest at the same height as your heart. This is the place where many people connect to their intuition.

6. Visualize that you establish a connection, like a telephone line, to your higher mind. Now send the idea to your higher mind, along with the question, What is a better understanding of this idea? Don't ask if the idea is true or false, and don't ask what to do in a particular situation. Your higher mind is not your inner psychic hotline. Instead, ask for a deeper understanding so that your conscious mind can make better choices.

7. Let go and relax. Perhaps use some kind of relaxation technique. If you do not already know a technique, visualize a scene that you consider peaceful and serene. It might be a sunset at the beach, where the waves gently lap ashore. It might be an early morning in the forest, where the birds joyfully greet the new day. Or it might be another place where you have had spiritual experiences in the past.

If you do not receive an answer, make a firm decision to move on without making an outer judgment about the idea. Simply remain open to the possibility that your higher mind might answer you later. When people are new to this technique, many find that they don't get an immediate answer. Instead, the answer comes later, often when they least expect it.

Make a decision that you will allow the process to run its course and that you will keep practicing. You will gradually become more comfortable with the technique, and this is the key to getting answers. To get answers you need to make room in your conscious mind for the answer to enter. The answer is already in your higher mind, and you need to invite it into your conscious mind.

In today's world, many people are so caught up in a stressful daily routine that they are not open to new ideas. Take a time-out and listen to the silence inside yourself. That silence can give you many golden answers.

DISCOURSE 2:
Everything Is Energy

One reason many people fail to get results from the path is that they do not take command over their inner circumstances. Therefore, it is helpful to understand the factors that prevent people from being in control of themselves.

The following discourses will describe the two most important factors that prevent you from improving your inner (and outer) circumstances. However, to clearly explain these factors, it is necessary to build a foundation that will clarify how the human psyche works. This discourse will use the latest discoveries of science to examine the question of whether people are more than just material beings.

A new world view is needed

Let us perform a thought experiment and mentally project ourselves back to medieval Europe. We find ourselves surrounded by people who believe the Earth is flat and that it is the center of the universe. For a person from the modern world, this is a somewhat shocking discovery. How could people possibly believe in ideas that are so obviously wrong? As we take a closer look, we find two reasons why people believe the Earth is flat:

- From early childhood, people are conditioned to believe the Earth is flat.

- Based on what people experience through their senses, it makes sense to say that the Earth is flat.

When you look towards the horizon, it seems reasonable that the Earth could be a flat disc and that you might fall off the edge. When you observe the night sky, it seems reasonable that the heavenly bodies are revolving around the Earth and therefore this planet must be the center of the universe.

As we take a closer look at medieval society, we realize that the belief in a flat Earth has a profound influence on people's view of themselves and their world. In reality, this belief is limiting people in many subtle ways, and it is preventing the progression of society as a whole. We clearly see that this incorrect belief has to go. Therefore, we get excited when a few scientists claim that the Earth is round and that it is not the center of the universe. We think, "Now we will see some major progress!"

To our dismay, the new scientific findings are not universally accepted. The new idea encounters fierce opposition from the powers that be and a general indifference from the people. At first, we feel stunned. How could people possibly reject a correct idea by clinging to old ideas that are so obviously incorrect? As we take a closer look, we realize that medieval people are not unintelligent or primitive. They are simply people, meaning that they are creatures of habit. Therefore, they are reluctant to let go of an idea that is familiar to them. As we watch the decades go by, we realize that it takes a long time before people change their world view according to the latest discoveries of science.

As we return to our own time, we feel a sense of relief. In today's world, people are no longer bound by outdated beliefs in a flat Earth. Then, a nagging question sneaks into our minds, "Are modern people really all that different?" The people of today are also creatures of habit. Is it possible that people still cling to outdated beliefs? What if modern people have not adjusted their world view based on the latest discoveries of science? Perhaps it might be helpful to take a closer look at scientific discoveries.

A relatively important discovery

During the 1800s, some scientists were talking about a phenomenon called "the end of science." Many scientists believed that existing scientific theories had explained all of the natural laws that created the material universe. Current theories could not account for a few things, but most scientists believed that these were "details," or "anomalies," that would soon be explained.

In 1903, a clerk at the Swiss patent office in Bern started studying one of these anomalies. While thinking about the problem, he had an intuitive vision that gave him a new view of how the universe works. It took him almost two years to translate this vision into a credible scientific theory. When he published his new theory in 1905, he quickly became world-famous. His name was Albert Einstein, and his new theory was the theory of relativity.

The theory of relativity shook the foundations of physics and opened new vistas for scientific investigation. Today, physicists still cannot fully explain all of the implications of this groundbreaking theory. Unfortunately, the theory of relativity has not had the same impact on the world view of the general population. The reason is that most people, including many scientists, have not understood or accepted the philosophical implications of this theory. Had these implications been generally accepted, an entirely new world view would have emerged.

If you are serious about making progress on the path, you cannot allow yourself to be limited by an outdated world view. Therefore, let us look at how the theory of relativity as well as other scientific discoveries can help you open up new opportunities for personal growth. As you consider the following ideas, please do not forget to use the inner approach to knowledge.

Unity behind diversity

When you examine the world through your senses, you discover an incredible diversity. Yet science has proven that this diversity exists only on the surface. When you go beyond the level of sensory experience, you discover greater unity and simplicity. All matter is made from molecules, and molecules are made from the combination of two or more different atoms.

Even atoms are not the final building blocks of matter. For decades, scientists believed that atoms were made of only three so-called elementary particles. After Einstein's discoveries, scientists found numerous subatomic particles, but even these particles are not the fundamental building blocks of matter. Scientists still have not developed a final theory of how matter is formed, but they do know that one cannot understand matter without understanding energy. In other words, energy is the deeper, underlying reality behind the diversity of so-called solid matter. The entire matter universe is built on a foundation of vibrating energy.

Breaking down barriers

The material world has many barriers that seem impenetrable to the senses. For centuries, people accepted the existence of an impenetrable barrier between the human mind and the human body. Before Einstein, physicists thought the universe was made from two separate elements, namely matter and energy. Although matter and energy could interact, they always remained separate, much like oil and water.

With his famous equation, $E=mc^2$, Einstein made this dualistic world view obsolete. His equation proves that matter and energy are not separate elements and that one can be converted into the other. Perhaps you were taught that a nuclear reactor converts matter into energy, but this explanation is not quite correct. A nuclear reactor simply frees the energy that is already stored in the atom. Energy is stored in the atom because matter is made from energy. Einstein's equation states that everything is energy.

Cause and effect

You have probably heard about the concept of cause and effect. For centuries, some scientists have attempted to explain every aspect of the universe as the effect of material causes. (For example, some scientists believe that thoughts are produced by chemical reactions in the brain.) As a result, many scientists have not yet begun to consider cause and effect in light of the fact that everything is energy.

Einstein's seemingly simple equation proves that there is more to cause and effect than meets the eye. If everything is energy, then energy is the underlying reality. Therefore, if we truly want to understand our observations of the matter world, we need to consider that a physical phenomenon could be the effect of a cause that takes place in a realm of energy. In other words, energy could be the cause, and matter could be the effect. Perhaps the entire matter universe is the effect of causes that occur in a deeper realm of pure energy.

The only difference is vibration

Although scientists know a lot about energy, they still cannot answer the question, What is energy? Instead, scientists talk about the properties of energy. The most distinct property of energy is that it vibrates. Energy moves in waves, and scientists talk about wavelength, amplitude and frequency. These words are simply different ways to describe and measure the vibration of energy.

The only difference between various forms of energy is a difference in vibration. You probably learned in school that visible light is light-energy and that various colors are created by light-energy of different frequencies. Violet light is not fundamentally different from red light; it merely vibrates at a higher rate. Furthermore, many forms of light are invisible to the human eye. Ultraviolet light vibrates too quickly and infrared light vibrates too slowly to be seen by the human eye.

Higher vibrations ↑	
High-frequency light	**Realm of pure energy**
Ultraviolet light	**Material universe**
Visible light	
Infrared light	

This points to two interesting facts:

- Your senses cannot detect certain forms of light, yet these forms of energy are as real as visible light rays or solid matter. Likewise, the realm of invisible energy is just as real as the matter universe.

- The only difference between various forms of light is in their vibration. Because so-called solid matter is a form of energy, it follows that the only difference between matter and less physical energy is a difference in vibration. Therefore, you can convert matter into energy, or energy into matter, by changing the vibration of the energy.

Going beyond matter

How valid is the idea of a realm, a dimension or a world made of pure energy? Scientists do not have final proof that such a realm exists, but they do have evidence. Based on Einstein's discovery, a group of physicists developed a new branch of science called quantum physics, or quantum mechanics. This science studies the world of subatomic particles, which is where matter meets energy. Because matter is made from energy, there must be a dividing line at which vibrating energy turns into solid matter.

Let us make this less abstract by visualizing that we take a trip into the deeper realms of matter. You know that your body is made from smaller building blocks called cells. Cells are made from even smaller entities, namely molecules. Molecules are made from atoms, and atoms are made from elementary particles that are incredibly small. Scientists have found that elementary particles are very different from what we normally consider a particle. In other words, elementary particles are not a bunch of tiny billiard balls moving around at the speed of light. In fact, scientists have discovered (and proven through numerous experiments) that elementary particles have a dual nature. Sometimes they behave as matter particles and sometimes they behave as waves of pure energy.

Higher vibrations	High-frequency or nonmaterial energy
Realm of pure energy	
Material universe	Material energy
	Subatomic particles
Lower vibrations	Visible matter

This discovery has baffled numerous physicists, but you don't have to be a rocket scientist to draw the logical conclusion. As you travel into the deeper levels of matter, you reach a dividing line. On one side of the line you find matter particles, and on the other side of the line you find pure energy. In other words, science has demonstrated that there is something beyond the matter universe. That something is a realm of pure energy.

How energy becomes matter

Quantum physicists devote their lives to studying the invisible world of subatomic particles/waves. They have developed huge instruments, called particle accelerators, to observe the subatomic world. These instruments have revealed how subatomic particles can collide and create new particles, and scientists are using these observations as the basis for figuring out how matter is formed. However, particle accelerators have also revealed a phenomenon which many present physicists consider an unimportant anomaly. Sometimes, a subatomic particle can literally appear out of nowhere.

Experiments show that a particle can appear and divide itself into several particles that travel some distance; then those particles collide and disappear back into the nowhere from which they came. What if this phenomenon turns out to be the key to taking quantum physics to a new level? What if such experiments prove that "matter" particles are the effects of an underlying cause which takes place in a realm of pure energy, a realm that is beyond the matter universe?

Some scientists have already formulated theories based on this possibility. These physicists talk about a "quantum field" or a "vacuum state" that lies beyond the horizon of the matter universe yet produces the entire universe. Will such ideas one day become mainstream science and empower humankind to develop a more complete world view?

Dark matter

While quantum physics studies the realm of minute particles, astrophysics studies the realm of solar systems and galaxies. Astrophysicists have discovered that the amount of matter in the universe cannot account for the gravitational pull that holds the universe together. In other words, if the universe was made exclusively from visible matter, the galaxies would long ago have drifted apart. In an attempt to explain this, some scientists have proposed the existence of so-called dark matter which is invisible to the human senses and (current) scientific instruments.

Where does dark matter exist? What if it exists in a realm that is beyond the matter universe yet connected to this universe? What if dark matter is actually pure energy, energy that is "invisible" from the matter universe? Perhaps we can find an underlying cause, existing in a realm of pure energy, which is holding the material universe together. Perhaps the matter universe is not a closed sphere but only one part of a larger whole. Albert Einstein talked about the "space-time continuum." Perhaps we need to consider that there may be a "matter-energy continuum" and that we cannot understand the material universe without understanding what lies beyond it.

How this relates to self-help

Today most people still cling to a dualistic world view and visualize a universe made from two separate elements. We have a solid element, called matter, and a fluid element, called energy. This dualistic world view is obviously based on the physical senses. Most people cling to this world view; however, science has proven that the human senses do not produce an accurate view of reality. In a scientific age, a world view based on sensory perception is almost as incomplete as the belief in a flat Earth.

If you are willing to leave this world view behind, you can make major progress on your personal path. You only need to adjust your world view to the scientific fact that you live in a world in which everything is energy. In reality, the concept of matter is inaccurate. Contrary to what your senses are telling you, the seemingly solid substance that you call matter is made from vibrating energy. Normally, you think of energy as a vibrating substance that is always moving. Yet this vibrating energy can be captured into a form, or matrix, that makes it appear as unchangeable matter. Scientists cannot yet fully explain how this happens, but the theory of relativity proves that it does happen.

What people call matter is not an actual substance. Matter is a mental concept that was created in the human mind. In reality, all matter is made from vibrating energy. Some of this energy appears solid to the human senses because the senses cannot detect the extremely fast vibrations of the energy that makes up so-called matter. Just think of how a rubber band or the string on a guitar can vibrate so quickly that you cannot see the individual vibrations but only a blur.

To fully accept a new world view, you might need to adjust your vocabulary. Instead of talking about matter and energy, you need to talk about "stationary energy" and "fluid energy." You also need to start visualizing that everything around you, no matter what your senses tell you, is made from vibrating energy.

Why is it so important to make this mental adjustment? Because by accepting that everything is energy, you can open up exciting new possibilities that will empower you to take control over your inner and outer circumstances.

Mind energy over matter energy

The previous discourse explained that the key to changing your outer situation is to first change your inner situation. We can now gain a different perspective on this idea.

Your inner situation is obviously the world of your mind and psyche. It should be obvious that your thoughts and feelings are not made of matter. Regardless of what you might believe about how thoughts and feelings are created, the thoughts and feelings themselves are not material substances but forms of energy. Hardly anyone disputes the existence of mental and emotional energy.

During most of recorded history, people have believed in the existence of a nonmaterial phenomenon called the soul. Only within the last couple of centuries have materialistic scientists disputed the existence of the soul. These scientists claim that all thoughts and feelings are the result of electrical and chemical processes that take place in the physical brain.

If this were true, then the entire concept of self-improvement would have no meaning. It could be reduced to an attempt to find a wonder drug or an electromagnetic device that would turn you into a perfect human being. If you were a hard-core materialist, you probably would not be reading this book. However, even materialists seem to recognize that thoughts and feelings are not material "things."In other words, they are forms of energy.

If you compare this to our previous considerations about the relationship between matter and energy, you might develop a new perspective on the existence of the soul. We have seen that matter does not produce energy. Although it is possible to convert matter into energy, this process simply frees the energy that is already stored in the matter substance. That energy is not produced by matter, because energy is the fundamental building block that is used to create matter in the first place. Therefore, the idea that the brain can create mental and emotional energy seems to contradict the discoveries of physics. A gross substance cannot produce the fundamental substance from which it was created. Water is made from oxygen and hydrogen atoms. Water does not produce the atoms; the atoms produce the water.

This does not mean that the chemical and electrical processes in the brain have no influence upon your thoughts or feelings. They obviously do, as demonstrated by scientific experiments and common experience. However, the fact that your brain can influence your thoughts does not prove that your brain produces those thoughts. You have probably seen an experiment that sends a beam of white light into a glass prism. The prism splits the white light into several light rays that have the colors of the rainbow. If you did not know that the white light entered the prism from an outside source, you might reason that the prism produced light of different colors. Likewise, if you define a theory which denies the existence of anything beyond the material universe, your only option is to reason that the brain produces thoughts.

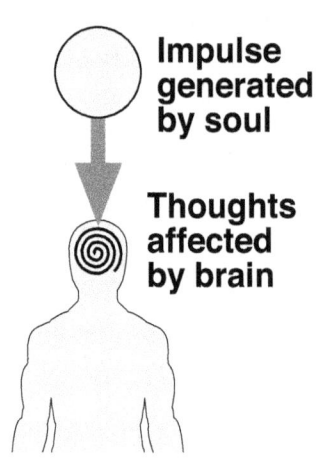

Impulse generated by soul

Thoughts affected by brain

Which came first, the brain or the soul?

If you are open to the idea that life might have a nonmaterial side, you might reason that thoughts are created by something that is beyond the brain. Thoughts are like the white light which the prism of the brain splits into various colors.

If the brain is not creating thought energy, then where are thoughts created? Could thought energy possible come from a more fundamental level of reality, a level of pure energy? Could it come from a nonmaterial entity that we might call the soul?

Currently, we cannot scientifically prove the existence of the soul. Yet neither do we have any way to disprove the existence of the soul. Consequently, the existence or nonexistence of the soul remains a matter of belief. To find your personal answer, why not apply the inner approach to knowledge?

Does it seem right to you that all of your mental and emotional processes are created by chemical reactions in the gray matter that happens to be deposited between your ears? Or does it seem logical that your thoughts and feelings originate at a level of reality that is deeper or more fundamental than the matter in the brain? Could it be that your thoughts and feelings originate at the level of pure energy and that they are produced by the soul? Could it be that the soul is not a product of the body but simply resides in the body for a season? In other words, the soul might be the cause and the body the effect.

Einstein's theory of relativity has proven that you are not a matter being but an energy being. If you want to understand your true identity, you must look beyond the matter sphere, or the material universe. Perhaps your body is a vehicle through which the soul interacts with the material world. If so, it follows that if you want to control your inner circumstance, you must first take possession of your soul. Perhaps the key to discovering your true identity might be hidden among the energy garments of your soul. In the following discourses, we will take a journey into the world of the soul.

DISCOURSE 3:
Overcoming Toxic Energies

At this point you might be thinking, "If I have to go through the trouble of developing a new world view based on the idea that everything is energy, then it sure would be nice to know what a new world view can do for me. What are the practical implications and how will it help me on my personal path?" The coming discourses will address this question.

We have already seen that to be successful on the path, you need to develop a deeper understanding of yourself and your situation. We can now see that this new understanding must incorporate the fact that energy affects every part of your life. As you develop a greater understanding of energy, you begin to see that every condition in your life can be understood in terms of energy. Your outer conditions are the effects of causes that are set in motion at a deeper level of reality, a level where everything is energy.

The most effective way to solve any problem is to remove the cause. If you will make an effort to learn how to free yourself from negative energy, you will be amazed at how seemingly insurmountable obstacles will suddenly start to disappear, much like the morning dew disappears under the rays of the rising sun.

The power of habit
By developing a better understanding of energy, you can gain a new perspective on one of the major factors that opposes your personal growth. Many people find it difficult to change their lives because they do not understand the existence of a

force in their own psychology which opposes change. This force is like a magnet that pulls you back into old patterns of behavior. We will later take a closer look at this force, but for now let us call it the force of habit.

Every human being has certain habits, and many of them are so subtle that they go unnoticed. Habit is not just a matter of outer behavior. Some types of emotional and mental habits affect the way you think and feel about yourself and about life. You also have a number of habits that determine how you respond to certain situations. Many people fail to realize that these mental and emotional habits often oppose their progress on the path.

Human beings tend to be creatures of habit. A habit is formed by repeating certain thoughts, feelings and actions until a pattern is created. After the pattern is created, a magnetic force pulls you into repeating that pattern over and over again. The more you repeat the habit, the stronger the magnetic pull becomes, and the more difficult it becomes to break the habit. You might say that your life has been locked in a groove, and every time you try to step out of that groove, some unseen force pulls you back.

What is this unseen force, or magnetism, that makes it so difficult to break a habit? What if it is an accumulation of energy in your subconscious mind. Such psychic energy might create a magnetic pull on your conscious mind and pull you into certain patterns of thoughts, feelings and actions. To fully explore this possibility, we need to once again look at some of the scientific findings about energy. However, let us first consider a visual image of this phenomenon.

Imagine that you get into your car to drive to work. You turn the key, put the car in gear, release the parking brake and step on the gas pedal. To your surprise, the car goes nowhere. The wheels are spinning on the pavement, yet you are not moving. The reason is that during the night someone placed a huge electromagnet behind your car. This magnet pulls your car backwards, and your engine cannot overcome the magnetic pull. You might be able to overcome the pull by revving up the engine. Obviously, this will put strain on the engine and cause you to use more gas. If you had to drive around all the time with a magnet pulling you backwards, you would probably wear out your car faster than normal. You would also waste a lot of money on gas.

The electromagnet that is pulling your car backwards can be compared to a negative habit. The magnetic pull is caused by an accumulation of energy in your subconscious mind, and this energy is preventing you from changing your life. You can look at this energy as a form of emotional energy that pulls on your feelings and gives you a desire to continue the habit. It can also be a form of mental energy that pulls your mind into thinking about a situation in a specific way, making you unable to find new solutions to old problems.

Obviously, many people start smoking because it fulfills an emotional desire. Once a habit is formed, emotional energy starts to accumulate in the subconscious mind, and this energy reinforces the emotional desire to smoke. In other words, to stop smoking you have to break both an emotional habit and a physical addiction. It will be far easier to break the physical addiction if you first break the emotional habit, because that habit undermines your resolve to change your behavior.

Many people find that when they try to break a negative habit, the magnetic pull is so strong that their willpower cannot overcome it. Other people manage to use their willpower and their intellect to suppress their emotional desire. While these people might succeed in changing their outer behavior, they have not actually freed themselves from the emotional pull of the habit. They might have to battle this magnetic pull for the rest of their lives, and it obviously puts strain on their emotional engine and causes them to waste emotional energy.

What would be the most effective way to deal with the magnet pulling your car backwards? Is it to rev up the engine in an attempt to overcome the pull of the magnet? Or would it be better to seek to understand the cause of the problem, and then switch off the power to the electromagnet? Some people are not willing to step back from their situation and consider the cause of their problems. They simply keep stepping on the gas until something breaks. If you are reading this, you are obviously not one of these people. You are willing to take an inner approach to life and look for the causes behind the effects. Therefore, let us move on to consider how you can turn off the power to the emotional magnet that pulls you into negative habits.

Your mind is an energy field

You are probably aware that your outer actions do not appear out of nowhere. Any action is the effect of a process that takes place in your mind, or psyche. If you want to change your actions, you must first change something inside your mind. Therefore, the key to any kind of personal change is to take control over your mind, or psyche. The first step towards doing this is to develop a deeper understanding of the mind itself. Let us consider the question, "What is the mind?"

Albert Einstein's theory of relativity made it clear that the human mind, like everything else in this universe, is made of energy. Scientists have discovered that energy is not always a wave traveling through space at the speed of light. Energy waves can be captured or organized into a pattern, or matrix. When energy waves are organized into a pattern, scientists talk about "standing waves" or energy fields.

During your school years, you might have seen the teacher place a bar magnet under a piece of paper and spread iron filings on top of the paper. As if by magic, the iron filings spontaneously organized themselves into a very distinct pattern of curved lines. You were probably told that the cause of this phenomenon is that the magnet creates an energy field around itself. The energy that is captured in the magnetic field moves along certain lines, and it pulls the iron filings into a distinct pattern. Obviously, this invisible energy field has a very real and tangible effect on visible matter.

Think about a magnet with a magnetic field around it and ask yourself, Does the magnet produce the magnetic field or does the field produce the magnet? When you consider the scientific fact that everything is energy, you might reason that it does not make sense to say that the gross matter of a stick of iron can produce the more fundamental energy that makes up the magnetic field. If people are caught in a sensory view of the world, they probably assume that the visible magnet creates the invisible field.

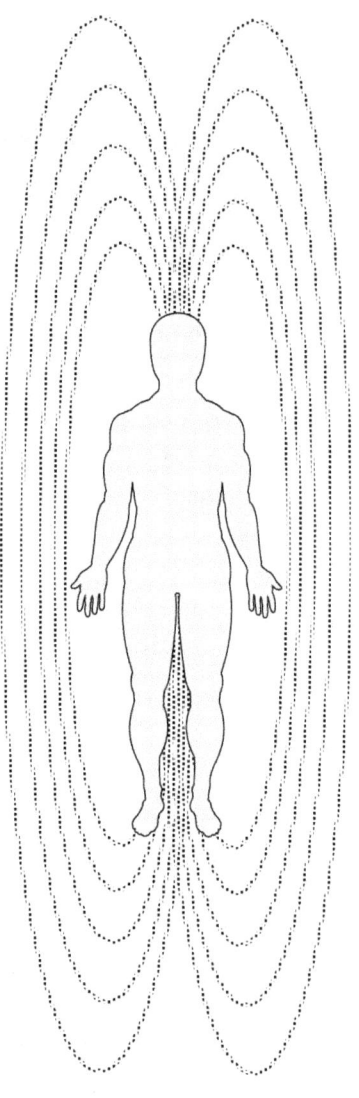

This reaction is exactly what caused medieval people to reason that the Earth was the center of the universe.

In reality, it must be the energy field that produces the material phenomenon which we perceive as a magnet. One might say that what we see as a stick of iron is simply the most dense part of the energy field. The energy waves of the field are so concentrated that our senses perceive them as solid matter.

To the end of his days, Albert Einstein was working on what he called a unified field theory. He was attempting to show that the entire material universe can be understood in terms of energy fields. Einstein did not complete his theory, yet the scientific facts do indicate that the entire universe is made from energy that is organized into fields.

It follows that the human mind is an energy field. You might visualize the mind as a container for energy. The mind is made up of mental and emotional energy which has been organized into a certain

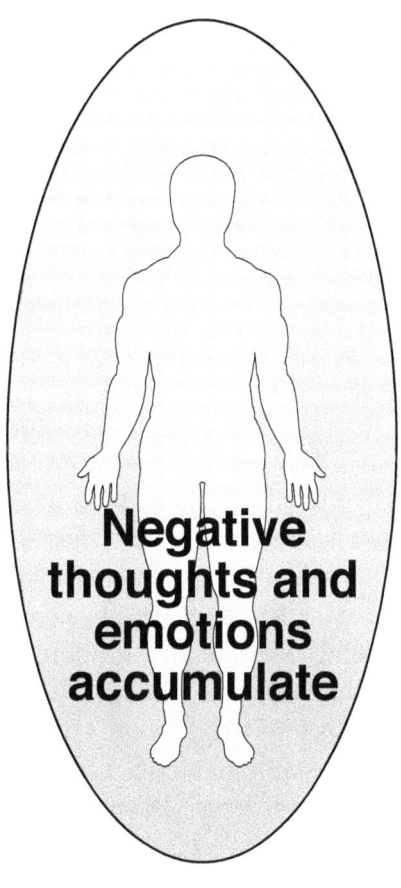

pattern, or matrix. A simple way to visualize your mind as an energy field is to compare it to the field that surrounds a magnet. Your mind can be visualized as an energy field that surrounds your physical body.

At this point, you might wonder if we can find scientific evidence for the existence of an energy field around your body, and indeed we can. Much research has been done about the electrical and magnetic properties of the human body, and some of it points to the existence of an electromagnetic field around the body. One researcher, Valerie Hunt at the University of California in Los Angeles, has spent decades researching the human energy field, and she has documented her findings in the book Infinite Mind.

Among other things, Valerie Hunt found that the energy waves in the field are connected to a person's mental and emotional state. People with a pessimistic or materialistic outlook on life tend to have a lot of low-frequency energy waves in their personal energy fields. People with a positive or spiritual outlook tend to have a lot of high-frequency energy waves in their fields.

In recent years, digital cameras connected to computers have been used to show visual images of the energy field surrounding the human body. Also, the science of acupuncture has recently become more accepted by Western doctors. This science is based on the idea of an energy field that affects the health of the physical body. As research continues, scientists will learn still more about the human energy field. Within a decade or two, the existence of a personal energy field is likely to become common knowledge, but you don't have to wait that long. You can use current scientific knowledge to increase your understanding of the energy field of your mind.

No energy field is an island

If your personal energy field is a storehouse for energy, then where does the energy come from? In the following discourse, we will see that some of the energy in your field comes from inside your own mind. However, your personal field is not isolated, and energy can flow into the field from outside sources. Your personal energy field is constantly exchanging energy with your surroundings. When you come into contact with other people, your energy field can interact with the energy fields of those people. In fact, because everything is energy, it follows that all of your interactions with the outside world can be described as exchanges of energy.

Once you realize that your mind is an energy field and that it is connected to an energy field surrounding your body, you gain an entirely new perspective on your interactions with the world around you. We have seen that all of your thoughts and feelings are forms of energy. Energy is characterized by the vibration, or frequency, of the energy waves. You have probably observed that certain thoughts or feelings can have a negative effect on your mental and emotional well-being. If another person becomes angry at you, it might make you feel angry or depressed. In reality, that person is directing certain mental and emotional energy waves at you. As these energy waves enter your personal energy field, they start affecting your state of mind, your life experience. Therefore, what you consciously experience as a negative emotion can be understood in terms of energy waves in your personal field.

One way to illustrate this is to compare it to your body. You know that certain chemical substances can have a negative effect on the chemical processes that are constantly occurring in your body. Some chemicals are toxic and can cause disease or even death. As you grow up, you learn to protect your body from toxic chemicals. Unfortunately, you have not learned to protect your mind from toxic energies.

What happens when you are exposed to negative emotional energy from others? Hatred is obviously a negative feeling, and love is a positive feeling. One difference between love and hatred is a difference in the vibration of the energy waves. One might envision that love is a high-frequency energy and that hatred is a low-frequency energy. You know that certain chemical substances will make your body stronger while other substances can kill your body. Similarly, high-frequency energy waves have a positive effect on your personal energy field and thereby on your sense of well-being. Low-frequency energy waves have a negative effect on your energy field. The logical conclusion is that if you are serious about personal progress, you need to learn how to protect your personal energy field from toxic energies just as you have learned to protect your body from toxic chemicals. You need to develop a form of mental and emotional self-defense, a sort of psychic karate. This becomes even more significant when we consider another scientific fact about energy.

Energy cannot be created or destroyed

One of the most fundamental laws of physics is called the first law of thermodynamics. This law states that energy cannot be created or destroyed. One form of energy can be converted into another form of energy, and this can be done by changing the vibration of the energy waves. The consequence is that energy will remain in a given state of vibration until it is transformed into a different state. Once an energy wave has attained a certain frequency, it will retain that frequency indefinitely or until something changes the vibration of the energy.

Consider that your personal energy field is a storehouse of energy. Your thoughts and feelings are forms of energy, and as you engage in certain mental and emotional patterns, you generate energy waves. Some of these energy waves can be stored in your field. As you interact with other people, mental and emotional energy enters your personal field, and some of it might remain in your field. The question now becomes, What happens to toxic mental and emotional energy after it has entered your personal energy field?

The first law of thermodynamics makes it clear that this energy will not simply disappear. It can remain in its current state of vibration for an indefinite period of time. Therefore, after toxic energy has entered your field, it will remain there until you do something about it.

You know that if your food contains certain chemicals, such as lead or mercury, these chemicals will accumulate in the cells of your body. While small amounts of these chemicals have no effect on your body, the accumulation can eventually reach a critical mass that leads to various forms of disease. What do you think happens when negative energy enters your personal energy field? Does it not seem logical that at least some of this energy will end up

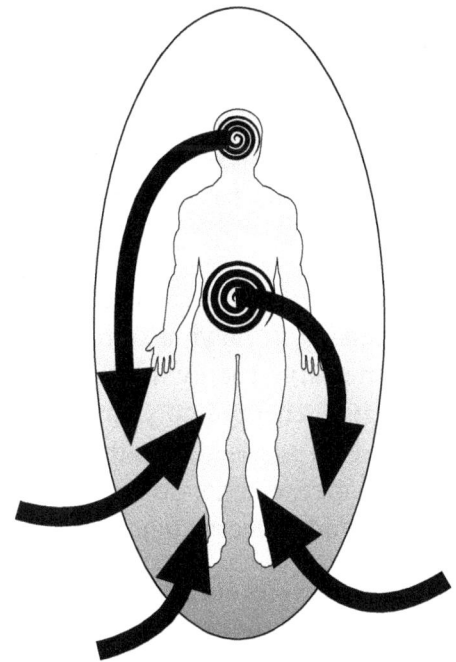

being stored in the field? As you grow older, more and more negative energy will accumulate in your field. After this accumulation reaches a critical mass, the energy can start affecting your mental and emotional well-being.

To understand how energy enters your field, we only need to consider the saying that Like Attracts Like. In reality, this saying refers to the law of gravity. Because we have now realized that everything is made of energy, we can gain a new perspective on gravity. Most people were taught in school that gravity is a force that affects matter. In other words, a large body of matter, such as the Earth, creates a gravitational force that pulls on all matter that comes near it. In reality, gravity is a force that is created by energy, and therefore it also affects energy. Einstein theorized that a large gravitational field would bend light waves, and this has been confirmed by scientific observations. Let us consider how this can affect you.

A self-destructive spiral

If you allow negative energy to accumulate in your personal energy field, that energy eventually reaches a critical mass that creates a gravitational pull. This has two potentially very negative effects:

- The gravitational force in your personal energy field will attract negative energy from your surroundings. In other words, the negative energy in your energy field pulls more negative energy into your field. Only very few people live in surroundings that are completely free from negative energy, so for most people there is plenty of negative energy to attract.

- The gravitational force in your energy field will have an internal effect on your thoughts and feelings.

Because you are not consciously aware of the stored energy, this energy must be stored in your subconscious mind. However, your conscious mind is also made of energy, and the gravitational pull of the energy that is stored in your subconscious mind can influence your conscious mind. The more negative energy you have stored in your personal energy field, the easier it becomes for you to become caught up in negative mental and emotional patterns.

When you put these two factors together, it becomes easy to see that you have the potential for the creation of a negative, or downward, spiral. As negative energy accumulates in your energy field, the gravitational pull causes you to engage

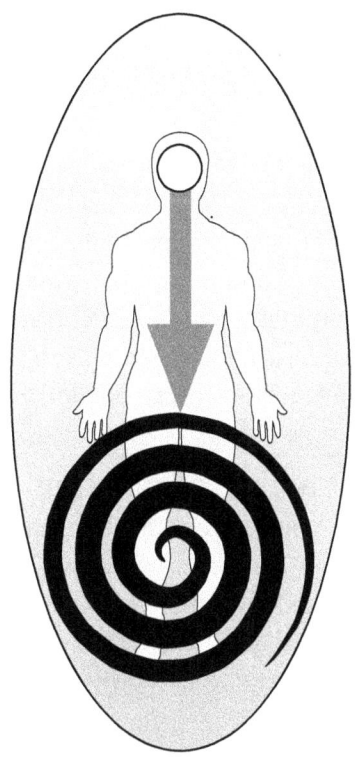

in negative thoughts and feelings, and this generates even more negative energy. Some of this energy is stored in your energy field, and it intensifies the gravitational pull. This gravitational pull also attracts more negative energy from your surroundings and every bit of it only adds to the force. The more negative energy you have in your energy field, the stronger the gravitational pull will be and the more negative energy will be generated and attracted.

In the beginning, the gravitational pull might cause you to engage in certain habits. They start as mental habits that affect the way you think about life. Then, they become emotional habits that affect the way you feel about life. Eventually, the mental and emotional habits give rise to certain patterns of behavior that affect what you do about life. At first, these habits might seem innocent, yet as the gravitational pull becomes stronger, it might reach a critical mass that overpowers your conscious mind. No matter how hard you try, you cannot use your willpower to pull yourself out of the negative habits. The gravitational pull of the negative energy has become so strong that it starts running your life.

You might visualize that as people allow negative energy to accumulate in their energy fields, the energy forms a maelstrom, or vortex, that pulls everything into itself. Perhaps you have heard about black holes in space. Perhaps you have seen film footage of a maelstrom in the ocean or a tornado over land. These phenomena are caused by matter swirling so quickly that it sucks everything into the vortex, and this is a visible illustration of what can happen in the invisible world of your personal energy field.

If you imagine that you have a raging tornado of negative energy in your personal energy field, it becomes obvious that this is an undesirable situation. If you have not yet reached this state, you need to make sure you never get there. If you are already caught in such a pattern, you need to make a determined effort to break the negative spiral.

Psychic or spiritual self-defense

If you are serious about the path, the idea that negative energy can form a downward spiral in your personal energy field is extremely important. Being forewarned is being forearmed. If you do not understand what is happening on an energy level, then you are likely to become a helpless victim of unknown forces. When you understand how energy affects you, you can do something about it.

When you consider the potential effects of having a maelstrom of negative energy raging in your subconscious mind, it becomes easy to see that this phenomenon is a major factor in almost every negative pattern of thoughts, feelings and behavior known to human beings. Your actions spring from feelings, and your feelings spring from thoughts. As negative energy begins to accumulate in your subconscious mind, the gravitational force of this energy starts affecting your thoughts. Your conscious thoughts are pulled into certain patterns that cause you to focus on undesirable or negative aspects of your life. If the gravitational force grows beyond a certain point, you will experience obsessive thoughts that you cannot willfully shut out of your conscious mind.

As the gravitational pull grows stronger, it starts to affect your feelings. Your feelings are pulled into negative and undesirable patterns. You might start getting irritable or edgy, and small events can cause you to lose your temper. You might start experiencing negative feelings about yourself, about certain aspects of your life or about life in general. If the gravitational force grows beyond a certain point, the negative feelings might overpower your conscious mind and prevent you from enjoying life. This is a state of mind that psychologists call depression.

As the negative energy keeps building, your personal energy field becomes a very unpleasant place to live. Unfortunately, your conscious mind has to live in your field. If your mind does not know how to remove the pressure of the negative energy, your mind will naturally start thinking about how to escape the pressure. As the intensity builds, your mind just wants to get away, and this leads to a desire for escape. One way to seek this escape is to dull the mind with a chemical substance, such as alcohol or drugs. Unfortunately, this does nothing to permanently remove the pressure, and it actually lowers your defenses so that more negative energy can be attracted. As the temporary relief wears off, the intensity returns with extra force, and it creates an even stronger desire for relief. This negative spiral can quickly become so intense that your conscious mind no longer has the strength to pull itself out of it. In extreme cases, it might give rise to the desire to end it all through the illusory escape of suicide.

Obviously, you can break such a negative spiral by learning how to protect yourself from the gravitational pull of psychic energy.

Breaking a habit

If you truly want to break any negative habit, including an addiction, you must begin by learning how to free yourself from the gravitational pull of negative psychic energy. Unless you reduce this negative pull, all other efforts to break a habit will be overpowered by the raging tornado of energy that roars through your personal field.

Throughout history, people have been wondering why they so often do things that their conscious minds do not want to do. Why do people feel compelled to do things that they know are harmful to themselves or to other people? Why do people engage in negative patterns that eventually lead to their own destruction? Why do some people find it impossible to pull out of such a destructive pattern? Why do some people become insensitive to the suffering of others? Why do some people become insensitive to their own impending destruction?

We can now answer all of these questions. The answer is that the negative energy in your personal energy field has created a gravitational pull so strong that it overpowers, or, one might say, consumes, your conscious mind. Often, a person's willpower is not strong enough to overcome the downward pull of the negative energy.

Overcoming denial

When people first hear that their lives might be controlled by a gravitational pull of psychic energy in their subconscious minds, they often react with disbelief or denial. Who likes to admit the existence of some uncontrollable force in their own mind? However, the eternal truth remains that denying the existence of a problem will not make that problem go away. And although the existence of a gravitational pull might seem like a heavy and depressing topic, it should truly be a cause for great hope and rejoicing.

A few hundred years ago, many diseases were considered incurable because people did not know what caused them. Then, scientists discovered bacteria and realized that these microorganisms cause many common diseases. Armed with this knowledge, scientists quickly discovered ways to kill harmful bacteria and thereby cure many diseases that had previously been considered incurable. Likewise, by acknowledging the effect of negative energies, you will be able to overcome many of the negative conditions in your life that have so far seemed like insurmountable obstacles. You simply need to learn how to build a spiritual defense against negative energies.

Defending your light

To build an effective spiritual defense, you need to learn how to do the following:

- Minimize the generation of negative energy by preventing yourself from engaging in negative thoughts, feelings and actions.

- Remove the negative energy that is already stored in your personal energy field.

- Create a shield around your energy field that keeps out the negative energy in your surroundings.

The concept of spiritual self-defense might be new to you, and therefore it might seem somewhat strange. However, to build an effective spiritual defense, you just need to continue and expand the mental retooling process that has been mentioned throughout this book. This is not nearly as difficult as it might seem. You can use the knowledge of how to defend the physical body and transfer it to the defense of your personal energy field. For most people, protecting the body has become second nature, and they often do things to take care of the body without even thinking about it. If you consider what you do to take care of your physical body, you will see that a lot of it applies to taking care of your "energy body."

You might think that because your personal energy field is invisible to your senses, it is more difficult to care for the field than your physical body. However, many of the things you do for the physical body are designed to defend it against invisible enemies. For example, you cannot see bacteria, but you know that if you leave food outside of the refrigerator, harmful bacteria start to form. You know that food or other substances can contain chemicals that are harmful to the body. You cannot see nuclear radiation, yet you probably would not select a nuclear waste site as the place for your next camping trip.

The many things you do to take care of the physical body have already become a natural part of your everyday life. For instance, when you cross the street, you automatically scan for approaching cars. If you will commit yourself to learning how to take care of your energy field, doing so will gradually become as natural as protecting your physical body. After an initial learning process, you will begin to defend your energy field without even thinking about it.

In discourse 6, we will look at specific techniques for building an effective spiritual defense. However, if you want to bring about real improvement in any aspect of life, you need to start by increasing your awareness. Increased awareness leads to greater understanding, and when you use common sense to apply that understanding, you have a strong foundation for producing positive change in your life. Therefore, let us consider how you can use common sense to defend your energy field.

Food, clothing and shelter for your energy field

To keep your body alive, you must feed it. However, to keep your body healthy and thereby keep it alive for a long time, you must feed it foods that contain the proper nutrition. This also applies to feeding your soul and your energy field. Many activities have a spiritual, or inspirational, effect on your mind and feelings. If such activities are not already part of your life, it would be beneficial to find one or more that appeal to you and incorporate them into your daily routine. Many activities can have a beneficial effect, but you only need to choose the ones that most appeal to you. This could be taking a walk or bike ride in a beautiful park, in a forest or along the beach. It could be reading spiritual or inspirational books or listening to uplifting music. Or it could be using various self-help or spiritual techniques.

To keep your body functioning well, you must give it the proper amount of rest. If you are running, your body will eventually get tired and you will naturally stop running. However, many of your daily activities can be so stressful that they get your thoughts and feelings running at high speed. People often get so caught up in these activities that they ignore the need to prevent their thoughts and feelings from running wild. It is essential to make a commitment to watch your mental and emotional state on a daily basis. If you feel that things are becoming so stressful that your thoughts and feelings start running wild, then you need to make a conscious decision to stop this negative spiral. You need to take a time-out and engage in activities that will give your thoughts and feelings a rest. You can use the activities mentioned in the previous section, because anything that feeds the soul will calm your thoughts and emotions.

You are probably not consciously aware of just how many things you do to defend your body against visible or invisible dangers. By increasing your awareness of how energy works, you will gradually begin to realize that just as your body is exposed to physical dangers, your energy field is exposed to many dangers on an energy level. When you realize that everything in this world is made of energy, you will understand that all human actions have an effect on an energy level. You can develop a sensitivity that allows you to feel which actions generate negative energy. Activities that disturb your sense of peace and harmony often generate toxic psychic energy. This has many implications, but let us look at just a few.

- Decades ago, no one realized that smoking had negative health effects. As awareness of the dangers of smoking has increased, many people have elected not to smoke. Likewise, as your awareness of negative energy increases, you can choose to avoid certain actions that cause you to generate or receive toxic energy.

Overcoming Toxic Energies

- You have probably run into people who are difficult to please. You might have noticed that the mere presence of certain people can make you feel agitated, uncomfortable or depressed. You can now see that such people might have allowed the accumulation of negative energy in their personal energy fields, and this energy has reached a critical mass that affects others around them. People can be radiating negative energy to such an extent that it can overpower others. We will shortly look at how you can defend yourself against such negative energy, but a commonsense precaution would be to avoid such people if you possibly can.

- So far, we have only talked about an energy field around your physical body, but in reality everything in the material world is made from energy fields. For example, a house has its own energy field, and this field can accumulate negative energy. Therefore, a physical location can have a large accumulation of negative energy, and this energy can be so strong that it forms a maelstrom, or vortex, that pulls you down. One way to identify such places is to consider what actions commonly occur in a given location. A constant repetition of negative, inharmonious or destructive actions will gradually create a vortex of negative energy. If you can identify such places, you have the option of avoiding them if at all possible.

- To keep your body healthy, you must keep it clean, and this has an inner and outer aspect. You must keep your body clean from dirt that clings to the outside of the body, and you must protect it from toxic substances that enter the body and might be stored in the cells.

- Likewise, negative energy can be directed at your energy field from outer sources, and it can cling to the field or enter deeply into the field. To keep your energy field clean, you need to employ specific techniques, and we will shortly consider such techniques. However, you can still do something by applying common sense. One obvious way to defend your energy field is to avoid people, places or activities that contain or generate negative energy. You would never even consider jumping into a sewer pond, yet many people inadvertently jump into a sewer pond of negative energy. It would be better to avoid following the fools who rush in where angels fear to tread.

- If your body has absorbed toxic chemicals, you can do various things to cleanse your body. Likewise, many activities will help you cleanse your field of toxic energy. Engaging in uplifting and inspirational activities will help cleanse your field, as will getting mental and emotional rest.

If you will make an effort to apply your new knowledge of energy to your daily activities, you will gradually increase your sensitivity to toxic energy. Just as you have developed an intuitive feel for potential danger to the physical body, you can develop a feel for dangerous energies.

No need for fear

As you increase your awareness of negative energy, you don't need to be afraid or paranoid about the existence of toxic energies. In discourse 6, we will see how you can defend yourself from the various energies in this world. However, to build such a psychic defense, you need to know that toxic energies exist, just as you need to know that bacteria exist before you can defend your body against their harmful effects. To avoid becoming fearful of negative energies, you need to do more than use common sense. You need to use specific techniques to defend yourself against the negative effects of harmful energies. This will be the topic of the following discourse.

DISCOURSE 4:
Building Your Energy Defense

This discourse will show you how to effectively defend your personal energy field by doing the following:

- Creating an energy shield around your personal field that prevents toxic energies from entering your field.

- Freeing yourself from the gravitational pull of toxic energies that are already stored in the field. To do this, you must learn how to transform or transmute toxic energies.

Because we have taken the time to build a greater understanding of energy, it becomes relatively easy to understand how you can accomplish these tasks. We simply need to take one more look at what scientists can tell us about the interaction of energy waves.

Imagine that you are standing next to a still pond. You throw a rock into the pond and circular waves start spreading from the point of impact. When the water becomes still again, you throw two rocks into the pond at the same time. Each rock creates a circular pattern of waves that spread from the point of impact. In the middle of the pond, the two wave patterns meet and an interesting phenomenon occurs. In the area that is affected by both wave patterns, the waves appear different from the original waves. When two wave patterns meet, the waves affect each other and create what scientists call an interference pattern. The visual image of waves on a pond illustrates what happens when invisible energy waves meet.

We have already seen that energy waves are characterized by their vibration, or what scientists call frequency, amplitude and wavelength. When two energy waves meet, the outcome of the interaction depends entirely on the vibrational properties of the two waves. If the waves have very different vibrations, the two waves will not create an interference pattern. They will either pass each other like ships in the night, or one wave might bounce off the other wave. In other words, the vibrations of the two waves will not be changed.

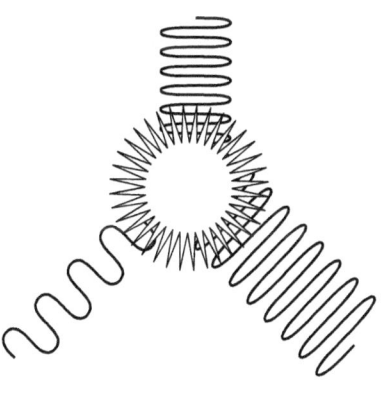

If the vibrations of the two waves fall within a certain range, the interaction will create an interference pattern. This interference pattern will create a new wave that is different from both of the original waves. In other words, both of the original waves will be changed, or transformed, into a different vibration. The new wave might have a lower vibration than one of the original waves and a higher vibration than the other wave. This phenomenon opens up amazing opportunities for those who are serious about personal progress.

We have seen that toxic energy is one of the major obstacles on one's personal path. Toxic energies have a lower vibration than beneficial energies, and this is what makes a spiritual defense possible. This has two profound implications:

- If you create a shield of high-frequency energy around your personal energy field, low-frequency energies from your surroundings will not be able to penetrate the shield. They will either bounce off the shield or be absorbed by (or transformed by) the energy in the shield.

- If you direct a beam of high-frequency energy into the toxic energy that is already stored in your energy field, you can raise the vibration of the toxic energy. You are, in a very real sense, transforming the low-frequency toxic energy into high-frequency energy.

Where can you find a source of high-frequency energy? With our present understanding of energy, we can easily answer this question.

The stream of energy

A previous discourse discussed the idea of a realm of pure energy beyond the material universe and a connection between this realm and the matter universe. Let us take a closer look at the scientific findings that relate to this topic.

As already mentioned, some of the experiments conducted by quantum physicists show that a subatomic particle can suddenly appear out of "nowhere." Some scientists have attempted to explain this phenomenon and they have come up with various theories. All of these explanations point to the existence of some aspect of reality beyond the material universe.

The findings of quantum physics seem to demonstrate that beyond the material universe is some other world, or field, in which energy exists in a different form than what can be seen in this world. Based on the previous discussion, one might say that beyond the material universe is a realm made of energies that have a higher vibration than the energies in the material world.

According to the physical senses, there is a barrier between the material universe and the energy universe. In reality, the only difference is in the vibration of the energy. A visual illustration of this could be the tonal scale. You might know that musical tones are divided into groups, called octaves. The only difference between a deep or high sound is in the vibration, or frequency, of the sound waves.

Likewise, one might say that the material universe is one octave in a larger whole, and beyond it we can find one or more octaves of pure energy. The only difference between the material octave and a higher octave is in the vibration of the energy waves. Therefore, energy can travel from a higher octave into the material octave. In fact, quantum physics seems to demonstrate the existence of a flow of energy from a higher octave into the material octave. That is why a matter particle can suddenly appear out of "nowhere" and disappear back into "nowhere." This particle does not come from nowhere; it comes from a higher octave through a process that lowers the vibrations of the energy wave. Once the frequency of the wave is lowered beyond a certain threshold, it becomes possible to perceive that energy with scientific instruments. When the vibration of the energy is lowered even more, the energy takes on the form of "solid" matter.

Science meets spirituality

To fully embrace these ideas, it may be helpful to use a specific term for the energy that belongs to the frequency spectrum that is above the material octave. We might call it high-frequency energy or spiritual energy.

Based on these observations, we must reason that the energy coming from a higher octave is a more fundamental energy than the energy perceived as material energy. In other words, the energies that are used to build the material world are low-vibration cousins of the higher energies. This is similar to the well-known fact that everything is made of molecules, which are made of atoms, which are made of subatomic particles. Therefore, one might consider that the entire material universe is made from high-frequency, spiritual energies that have been lowered in vibration. These ideas seem to indicate that the most advanced field of modern physics points towards a world view that spiritual people have held for thousands of years.

The findings of quantum physics are so different from a materialistic world view that scientists find it difficult to use normal metaphors or images to explain these findings. In an attempt to find explanations, some scientists have compared the findings of physics to some of the spiritual teachings found on this planet. Several books have been written on this topic, including the classic The Tao of Physics by Fritjof Capra.

Higher vibrations	
Spiritual realm	**Spiritual energy**
Material universe	**Material energy**
	Subatomic particles
Lower vibrations	**Visible matter**

By comparing quantum physics to spiritual teachings, we can envision that the material universe is part of a larger whole and that beyond this universe are spiritual worlds. The material world is an extension of the spiritual worlds. In fact, you may want to adjust your way of thinking and consider that you live in a small part of a spirit-matter continuum. The material world is the visible part of this continuum, and we might compare it to the tip of an iceberg. You know that an iceberg has 90 percent of its mass under water, and likewise the majority of the spirit-matter continuum is hidden from view.

The material world can only exist because the light-energy that makes up the spiritual worlds is lowered in vibration until it becomes material energy. In other words, the entire material universe is made up of spiritual energy that has only temporarily been lowered in vibration. So the material world can only continue to exist because of a constant stream of high-frequency energy.

The logical conclusion is that if you want to get the high-frequency energy needed for a spiritual defense, you must get it from a higher octave. You simply need to reach up into that octave and pull the spiritual energy into your personal energy field. How can you draw spiritual energy into the material octave? Fortunately, the answer is readily available.

Mind over matter?

For centuries, people in both scientific and religious circles have debated the relationship between mind and matter. We can now gain a better understanding of this question by considering the following ideas:

- Beyond the material world is at least one world, or octave.

- Energy flows from this higher octave into the material octave.

- The energy from the higher octave is what coalesces into material energy and matter.

Science cannot explain how this process occurs, but quantum physics seems to demonstrate that your consciousness has the capacity to be part of the process.

One of the cornerstones of quantum mechanics is the so-called uncertainty principle, which demonstrates that you cannot predict the outcome of a subatomic experiment or event. Physicists have found that whenever they conduct an experiment that involves subatomic particles, a number of potential results exist. These potential results do not exist as actual events; they exist in what is called the realm of probability.

In light of the idea that there is something beyond this universe, one might say that the octave that is immediately above the material octave is an octave made of energy that does not have material form (it has a higher vibration than the energy in the material octave). However, this spiritual energy has the potential to take on form.

When a physicist conducts an experiment, one might imagine the existence of ten potential results. As the experiment takes place, one of these potentialities will become actualized as an event that can be observed in the material world. Scientists cannot yet explain how one of the potential results is selected over the others. However, quantum physics has demonstrated that the outcome of the experiment is a product of what scientists call the entire measurement situation. This situation normally has three elements:

- The phenomenon that is being observed, such as a subatomic event

- The instruments used to observe the phenomenon, such as a particle accelerator

- The mind, or consciousness, of the observer

The result of the experiment is a product of the interaction of all three elements—including the consciousness of the scientist. The implications of this discovery are nothing short of staggering, yet many scientists have been extremely reluctant to consider the philosophical implications. The reason is that one of the cornerstones of science is that scientific observations are objective, meaning that they are not influenced by the consciousness of the scientists. Quantum physics seems to invalidate this claim, and that could force scientists to reevaluate everything. Because scientists are also creatures of habit, most of them are reluctant to rethink familiar ideas. Nevertheless, a new scientific paradigm will eventually emerge. If you are willing to apply the inner approach to knowledge, you do not have to wait for that to happen.

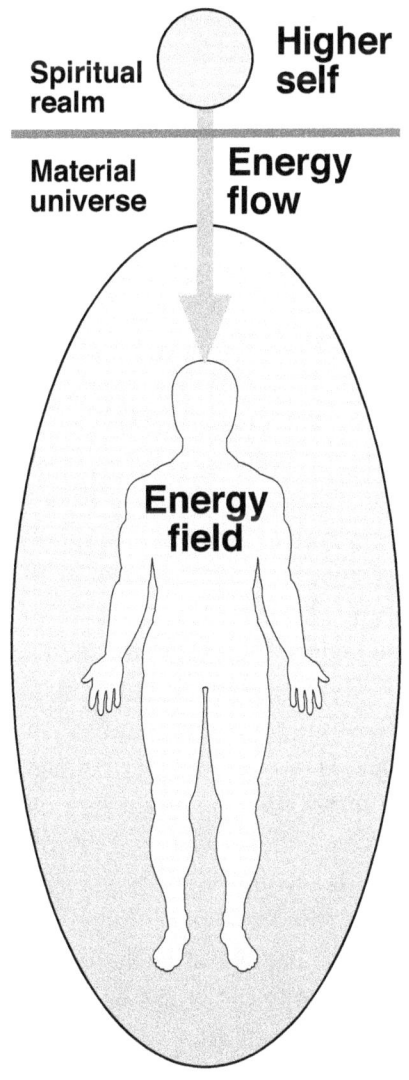

One of the implications of the uncertainty principle is that your consciousness has the potential to interact with the octave that exists immediately above the material octave. Your mind can reach beyond the material octave, and it can act as a conduit that allows high-frequency spiritual energy to flow into the material world.

Once again, this has an obvious parallel to what spiritual teachings have been saying since the beginning of time. Virtually every spiritual or religious teaching originated because one person had an inner, spiritual vision of a realm beyond the material world. Let us take a closer look at this phenomenon.

Visions of other worlds

Throughout the ages, numerous people have claimed that they have had visions of worlds beyond the material universe. Such visions are found in every society, in every culture and in every historical period.

In the present time, such visions have become more common because of the advances of medical science. Today, many people are brought back to normal consciousness after the physical body is pronounced dead. Many of them experience that some aspect of their consciousness leaves the physical body and travels into a world that is different from the material world, yet it seems as real as this world.

By definition, a materialistic scientist is one who denies the validity of any kind of spiritual or near-death experience. However, if other octaves do exist, as modern physics indicates, then it might be possible for the human mind to perceive these worlds. Obviously, people cannot see these worlds through their physical senses. However, if the mind is set free from the influence of the physical senses, as appears to happen after the death of the physical body, then it might be possible and even natural to "see" what is not visible to the senses.

The radio of the mind

This opens up an interesting perspective on the human mind. The atmosphere around you is constantly being traversed by radio waves that you cannot perceive with your physical senses. However, by using an instrument called a radio, it becomes possible for you to make these waves "visible" to your sense of hearing. You are, so to speak, bringing the inaudible radio waves into the audible realm. Different forms of radio waves are separated only by their frequency. By turning a dial on the radio, you can tune in to radio waves of different frequencies, which you experience as different radio stations.

We have seen that everything is energy and that various forms of energy are separated only by their vibration. Therefore, we can find no impenetrable barrier between the material octave and higher octaves. All worlds are made of the same basic substance, namely energy. The higher octaves are different levels of vibration that exist alongside the material world. In other words, just as your living room is traversed by radio waves, the material world exists in the same "space" as the invisible octaves.

Spiritual visions indicate that the human mind has the capacity to act in a way similar to a radio. By turning the dial of consciousness, it becomes possible to tune in to energy frequencies that are beyond the frequencies of the material octave. Thereby it becomes possible, not with your physical senses but with your inner, or spiritual, senses, to perceive worlds beyond this one.

Throughout history, such extrasensory perception has happened to numerous people. A neutral observer will find a substantial body of evidence that points to the existence of worlds beyond the material universe. A hard-core materialist, will probably reject this evidence without giving it open-minded consideration. However, if you are willing to consider this evidence and apply the inner approach to knowledge, you can establish a foundation for taking a major leap forward on your personal path.

Let us return to the idea that to build an effective spiritual defense, you need to find a source of high-frequency energy. We have seen that the place to find this energy is in the octave that is right above the material octave. You also need to find a way to bring this energy into your personal energy field. What if the ability to do this is already built into your being? In other words, building a spiritual defense is not a matter of learning some kind of magic or sorcery. You already have everything you need to build this defense. You just need to become consciously aware of your abilities and to start using them in the most efficient way possible.

But how could you do this? Learn how to invoke spiritual light and then put it to work for yourself! This is not a supernatural ability that is somehow reserved for the few. All people have this ability. It is your spiritual birthright!

The higher mind

Before we consider specific techniques for invoking light, let us briefly consider why you have the ability to do so. Consider the image of an iceberg which has only a small part of its total mass above the water. Psychologists do not yet know everything about the human mind, but they all agree to the existence of multiple layers, or levels. The psychologist Carl Jung was the first to speculate that the human mind has a higher part, which he called the superego. In recent decades, many other psychologists have formulated similar ideas about a higher self, which is the seat of your intuitive and spiritual faculties. The idea of a higher, or spiritual self, is also part of the spiritual, metaphysical and esoteric traditions found in many parts of the world, including the West.

Building Your Energy Defense

What if your conscious mind, and even what is normally called the subconscious mind, make up only the tip of the iceberg of your total being? In light of our new understanding of energy, it seems necessary to develop a new way to look at the human mind. Perhaps the reason why the human mind has the ability to experience higher octaves is that part of it is constantly abiding in those octaves?

Could it be that what is normally called consciousness is a small part of your being, a part that vibrates within the spectrum of the material octave? Beyond this part of your being, we might find other parts of your being which are made up of energy that vibrates within the spectrum of a higher octave. In other words, your total being has its own personal spirit-matter continuum. A part of your being abides in higher octaves, and another part abides in the material octave. We might say that your true identity, your true being, is the higher mind, which has its permanent home in higher octaves. Your soul is an extension of the higher mind, and she is visiting this world only temporarily.

Higher vibrations	
Higher vibrations Spiritual realm	**Higher mind**
Material universe	**Higher subconscious mind**
	Conscious mind
Lower vibrations	**Lower subconscious mind**

We stated earlier that you have the ability to go within and discern true ideas. Obviously, this ability must come from the higher mind. If this mind resides in a higher octave, it follows that it would be above and beyond the lower energies that cloud your vision in this world. Therefore, this higher mind can see reality without the filter of the outer consciousness or senses. Does it not seem logical that by contacting your higher mind you could receive invaluable insights that could help you discern the right course on your personal path? If you will openly contemplate these ideas, you can make major progress towards understanding who you truly are.

We will take a closer look at these ideas in part two and go into great detail with the anatomy of your total being. For now, let us consider the idea that the reason you can access and draw forth spiritual light is that a part of your being is anchored in a higher octave. This creates a connection between your conscious mind and the higher octave. You simply need to become aware of this connection and open up a conduit for spiritual light. Through a perfectly natural process, spiritual light flows into this octave, and some of it flows through your mind. Consequently, expanding your ability to draw forth and direct spiritual light is a normal activity for a human being. You are, so to speak, designed to do this.

The mind is constantly creating

Some people realize the existence of toxic energy, but they cannot quite accept that they can personally transmute this energy. How could the human mind possibly transform this invisible energy? The answer is that what the mind has created, it can also uncreate.

The mind creates toxic energy by lowering the vibration of spiritual energy. The mind can also raise the vibration of toxic energy by directing spiritual energy into it. Once you begin to contemplate the scientific aspects of energy, it quickly becomes clear that these ideas are not mystical or abstract. Human beings have the ability to pollute water, but they also have the ability to restore that water to its original purity. For centuries, people polluted water but they had not developed the understanding of how to purify it. Likewise, people have been producing toxic energy. Now we know that we have the ability to purify this energy and thereby overcome the negative effects of toxic energy.

Using self-help techniques

How do you invoke and direct spiritual light? Because this is a natural ability, you can do it in many different ways. However, most people find that they get the best results by using some kind of self-help technique or spiritual technique. Where can you find such a technique?

By incorporating scientific discoveries about the nature of energy, these discourses seek to present a new and better understanding of the personal or spiritual path. Obviously, this understanding could not have been presented a century ago. However, the universe was still made of energy before people realized that it was so, just as the Earth was round when people believed it was flat. Therefore, humankind has faced the problem of toxic energy since the beginning of time. Over the centuries, people have found many different ways to build a spiritual defense. In the past, such techniques were generally given forth in a spiritual or religious context. In recent decades, we have seen an increased interest in a universal approach to personal growth. Therefore, you can find many different techniques in the field of self-help or self-improvement.

How do you find a technique that is right for you? Consider the following ideas.

- If you prefer an approach that is not religious or spiritual, you can find numerous books or organizations that offer self-help techniques, many of which are suitable for invoking light. The selection is so large that any person with an open mind is likely to find something that appeals to him or her. The bibliography of this book contains several references to books that present self-help techniques.

- Do you consider yourself as belonging to a particular religion? If so, you will probably find that your religion has several rituals or techniques that will help you invoke spiritual light. Perhaps you have never thought of or heard about these rituals as ways to invoke spiritual light. However, if you will practice a ritual with the intent to invoke light, you will probably find that the ritual takes on an entirely new meaning.

- Are you open to the spiritual side of life but do not feel that you belong to one particular religion? If so, you might look for spiritual techniques in several different religious and spiritual contexts. If you are truly open to trying something new, you will discover a large variety of techniques and rituals, and you are likely to find something that will appeal to you.

Selecting a spiritual technique

If you have never practiced any spiritual or self-help technique, the task of finding a suitable one might seem overwhelming and confusing. In reality, it is not. Consider the saying, "Ask and you shall receive!" Try to open your mind and truly seek for a technique by applying the inner approach to knowledge. If you will listen for an answer coming from inside yourself, you will find a technique that will work for you. In discourse 6, you will find an exercise that will make it easier for you to find a technique and to find answers to any question you might have about the path.

This book will suggest various techniques that might be helpful to you. However, these discourses are not meant to elevate one technique over others or to say that everybody should use the same technique. In selecting a technique, you must remember that you are a unique individual. What works for someone else might not work for you. And then again, it might. The ultimate way to select a technique is to apply the inner approach to knowledge. Your higher self already knows which technique is best for you right now. You just need to draw that answer into your conscious awareness.

In contemplating which technique to use, look for one that appeals to you in your present state of consciousness. However, keep in mind that as your understanding grows, you might benefit from finding a different technique or supplementary ones. A specific technique might be useful only for a time. It might help you climb to a certain level on the path, but once you are at that level, you might need another technique. Therefore, it is wise not to become rigid in your use of a technique, not to fall into the trap of thinking that if only you practice a particular technique for the rest of your life, you will automatically be saved. It is better to continue to use the inner approach to knowledge, and let your higher self tell you when it is time to move on.

To select a technique, it might be helpful to know the different types of techniques that are available.

Meditation
Meditation helps you focus your attention inside yourself and lose your awareness of the outside world. You can find many forms of meditation, but keep in mind that a primary

purpose of meditation is to help you gain conscious contact with your higher self. Meditation in itself will not necessarily help you invoke light, but it can help you develop attunement with your higher self. Once you have this attunement, you can use other techniques to draw forth and direct the spiritual light.

Some meditation techniques are aimed at helping you empty your mind of all thoughts. In today's world, there is much negative energy in the environment, and nature abhors a vacuum. An empty mind can easily become a target for negative energy. Therefore, it is generally safer to use a type of meditation that does not seek to empty your mind. Instead, you can focus your attention on something inside of you—your higher self.

Some of the most efficient meditation techniques are breathing exercises and many books on yoga contain descriptions of such techniques.

Prayer

If you believe in the power of prayer, it can be a powerful way to invoke light. The effect of prayer is in direct proportion to your faith in its power. If you believe in God, you probably think of God as a being who is beyond this world. Most people believe that God resides in a higher realm. Based on the previous ideas about spiritual energy, you might consider that God can send spiritual light into this octave in response to your prayers. If you believe in the existence of spiritual beings, such as Jesus or Buddha, such beings also reside in higher octaves. Therefore, they too can send spiritual light into your world in response to your prayers. If you do not feel comfortable praying to God or to a religious figure, consider praying to your higher self.

When praying, be as specific as possible. You can pray for God to send forth spiritual light to protect you from all toxic energies. You can pray for spiritual light to transform all toxic energies in your personal energy field or in the world around you.

Visualization

Visualization is a technique whereby you start by going inside yourself and establishing attunement with your higher self. You then visualize spiritual light streaming forth from your higher self into this octave, and you can direct that light into specific conditions that you want to change. As you will see later, visualization is an efficient way to build a spiritual defense. You can find many forms of visualization, and one specific technique will be presented in discourse 6.

Affirmations

This is a technique whereby you affirm a specific condition as if it is already manifest in your world. For example, you can affirm that you are protected by a shield of impenetrable spiritual light. Or you can affirm that spiritual light transmutes all darkness in your being. You can repeat an affirmation silently inside your head, but you will gain a much more powerful effect by speaking it aloud. In discourse 6, several affirmations will be presented.

Spiritual rituals

Many rituals can help you invoke light, especially if you perform them with attunement to your higher self. Most religions have specific rituals or techniques that were originally designed to help people bring forth light. In many cases, the original purpose behind these rituals has been forgotten, and few people understand their potential value. If you already practice such rituals or have done so in the past, consider applying those rituals for the purpose of bringing forth spiritual light from your higher self. You will be amazed at the results.

If you have never practiced a ritual, try to find one that will appeal to you. If you adhere to a particular religion, look within that context. For example, giving a rosary to the Virgin Mary is an efficient way to invoke spiritual light. Or try to read aloud your favorite religious scriptures while visualizing a stream of spiritual light flowing into this octave through the words.

If you do not follow a specific religious faith, you might want to look for rituals that are presented in a more universal context. Many people have discovered the value of yoga or breathing exercises that originated in the East. Several Eastern techniques, such as tai chi, are designed to help you direct spiritual energy. Walking a labyrinth is another possibility that has become popular in recent decades. Physical exercise can be used as a way to bring spiritual light into the physical body. Listening to inspirational or spiritual music can also have an effect. Certain classical music, such as Handel's Messiah, can help you invoke spiritual light, as can Gregorian chants. In some nations, such as India, there is an old tradition for using music or religious chants to invoke spiritual light.

Tips for practicing a spiritual technique

During recent decades, many people have tried to use spiritual techniques or self-help techniques as a way to accelerate their personal growth, and many have been disappointed over the lack of results. The reason for the missing results is not necessarily flaws in the techniques being used. The most

Building Your Energy Defense 87

common explanation is that people do not understand how to practice and apply a spiritual technique.

In the Western world, most people have grown up around technology, and they take it for granted. Many are so used to mechanical devices that they think the spiritual path can be approached in a mechanical way. These people suffer from a phenomenon which we might call the "push-button mentality." When you go into a dark room and flip a little switch on the wall, you expect the light to turn on. Likewise, when people become aware of the need to bring light into the dark dungeons of their own consciousness, they often think that a spiritual technique should work as a mechanical device. In other words, if they sit down and practice a technique, the light should automatically turn on. Unfortunately, this is not the case!

If you approach a spiritual technique as if it were a mechanical device, you will not receive the full benefit of that technique. Practicing a spiritual technique is not a mechanical process but rather an artistic process. The results depend on how you perform the technique.

Though some spiritual techniques are so powerful that they will produce effects no matter how you perform them, even these will be much more efficient if you perform them in the correct manner. This involves the following elements:

- Clarity of purpose. It is important to realize that the true purpose of a spiritual technique is to bring forth spiritual light from a higher octave. This light can only come from your higher self or from a spiritual being residing in that octave.

- Inner attunement. To bring forth spiritual light, you need to first establish a connection between your conscious mind and the source of that light. Imagine that a person builds a house and installs the entire electrical system. The person now flips a switch, but the light does not turn on because the electrical system of the house has not yet been connected to the grid. In reality, many people practice a spiritual technique without establishing a connection to the source of the spiritual light. That source is, of course, your higher self or a particular spiritual being.

• Accuracy in application. After you establish a connection to the source of the spiritual light, you can direct that light into conditions where you want the light to produce positive change. Imagine that you are washing your car with a garden hose and use a fine mist that covers the entire car. This fine mist might wash off some of the surface dirt, but it will not get the caked mud. To remove the mud, you must concentrate the beam of the hose and direct it at specific locations. This also applies to invoking light. You will always benefit from invoking light, but you will experience a much greater effect by directing a concentrated beam of light into specific conditions.

Types of spiritual light

Many spiritual teachings talk about different types of spiritual light. The easiest way to illustrate the different forms of light is to describe the light in terms of visible colors. The following is a brief description of various types of spiritual light.

• Blue and electric blue light. The blue light is especially suited for protecting you against any type of negative energy or even against negative physical conditions. Visualize a shield of intense blue light around your personal energy field.

• Golden yellow light. Golden light carries the properties of illumination and understanding. Visualize golden light in or around your brain and mind to raise your understanding of a particular issue. Visualize the golden light penetrating and illumining a specific idea or situation that you want to understand.

• Pink light. Pink light carries the vibration of love. Love is an extremely powerful vibration that consumes all unlike itself. Visualize an intense flame of love that consumes all anger and hatred in your own being or in other people.

• White light. This is the light of purity. White light has a very high vibration, and a shield of white light around your energy field can repel all lower energies. White light can also be directed into pockets of toxic energy in your field or in your surroundings. Visualize white light as being very intense, much like the color of the sun shining upon fresh snow.

• Emerald green light. This is the flame of healing, and it has the power to restore all imperfect manifestations to their original design. Emerald light is especially suited for healing the physical body. Visualize an intense flame of emerald green surrounding and penetrating any imperfect condition in your body.

• Purple light. This light carries the flame of peace and it can consume all inharmony. Visualize purple light surrounding any condition in your life that disturbs your inner peace and harmony. If you get angry or agitated, visualize a spinning disc of purple light over your solar plexus area.

- Violet light. On the scale of visible light, violet light has the highest vibration, and just above it is ultraviolet light. The spiritual form of violet light has a vibration that is very close to the energies in the material octave. Therefore, violet light is especially efficient for transforming toxic energies into a higher form of energy. Visualize a violet flame in and around any form of negative energy or condition in your life. See how the light transforms all lower energy into a higher form of energy.

As you will see in part two, the grand design of this universe took into consideration that people might misqualify energy and thereby become entrapped by the gravitational pull of that energy. Therefore, a safety mechanism was built into the system. That safety mechanism is that low-frequency energy can be purified by coming into contact with high-frequency energy. When you want to purify misqualified energy, the most effective form of spiritual energy is the one that vibrates right above the frequency spectrum of the material universe.

This form of spiritual energy has been used by spiritually minded people in every culture and time period. It has been known and referred to by many names, such as "grace," the "Holy Spirit" and the "cosmic eraser." Virtually every spiritual or religious organization has rituals that invoke and direct this form of energy (even if no one realizes the true purpose of these rituals).

During the past century, some spiritual organizations have referred to this form of energy as the "Violet Flame." Several organizations provide detailed teachings about this form of energy as well as detailed techniques for using it to transform toxic energy. A number of spiritual techniques are available for free at www.askrealjesus.com in the Personal Growth section.

DISCOURSE 5:
Making Truly Free Choices

These discourses are designed to help you overcome the limitations that prevent so many people from making progress on the path. So far, we have considered several factors, but we will now look at the one factor that will make or break your self-help efforts. To make maximum progress on the path, it is essential that you understand how this one factor influences every aspect of your life. Unfortunately, many people, including many psychologists and self-help experts, do not adequately consider this factor. The factor in question is your free will.

For centuries, religious scholars, philosophers and scientists have been debating the existence of free will. Some religious scholars claim that human beings cannot have free will, because everything in this world is subject to the will of God. Some scientists claim that the entire universe is like a large machine and that everything is determined by the laws of nature. Philosophers tend to go into complex arguments for or against the existence of free will. We need not go into the complexities of these arguments, because anyone willing to apply the inner approach to knowledge will quickly realize that human beings do indeed have free will. You probably don't have someone forcing you to read this book. You made the choice to start reading it, and after every sentence you choose whether or not you will keep reading. Every time you come across an idea that seems to go beyond your existing beliefs, you choose how to react to that idea. Will you make a decision with your outer mind, or will you apply the inner approach to knowledge?

Are you using your free will?
The essential question about free will is not whether you have it but whether you are using it. At any given moment you are making choices. But are you making truly free choices or are you allowing those choices to be made for you? Two conditions must be fulfilled before you can make a truly free choice:

- You must make the decision with your conscious mind.

- You must base your decision on a complete understanding of the situation.

The reason so many people do not make maximum progress on the path is that they have not made an effort to take back their ability to make truly free choices. Many people allow their subconscious minds to make choices for them, or they make conscious choices without having right understanding of the situation. How many times have you heard people try to justify something by saying, "I had no other choice!" If you really had no other options, you didn't actually have a choice. To make a choice, you must have more than one option. If you, inside your mind, believed that there was only one thing to do, then you were not making a choice. You were forced into acting a certain way and something had suspended your free will. However, is it really true that you sometimes have no options?

Free will is a gift
The gift of free will is the most profound gift that humankind has ever received. Using your free will is your divine birthright, and it is also your supreme personal responsibility. The idea that you could possibly be in a situation where

you "had no choice" is and always will be an illusion. You always have choices. You never have only one possible way to react. If you believe so, then you have allowed your outer mind to become manipulated either by forces outside yourself or by forces in your own subconscious mind. You have given up your personal responsibility to choose.

Earlier we talked about the equation of life and stated that some people see themselves as victims of their outer circumstances or of other people. If you allow yourself to think you are a victim, you give up your ability to choose how to react to a given situation. When you accept the expanded equation of life and realize that your inner circumstance has a major impact on your life experience, you see that the key to taking control over your inner circumstance is to learn to make better choices. Learning to make better choices means that you must draw the decision-making process into your conscious mind and seek to base your choices on right understanding. If you do not have the full understanding of a situation, you cannot make a truly free choice. The way to get right understanding is to apply the inner approach to knowledge and thereby get understanding from your higher self.

Let us take a closer look at the two factors that will help you take back your free will.

The subconscious computer

Some scientists believe that the human mind is nothing more than a sophisticated computer and that they will eventually construct a computer with the same intelligence as human beings. These discourses are not meant to imply that the human mind is a computer. However, a certain element of the human mind, namely the subconscious mind, functions in ways that are similar to a computer. Therefore, we will use the metaphor of a computer to explain some of the functions of the subconscious mind without thereby equating you with a computer.

A computer, of course, is a mechanical device and does not have intelligence or a will of its own. If you get into your car and push a certain button, the headlights turn on. Likewise, to make the computer do something, you must click a button on the screen. However, you can set up your computer to do certain things without having direct input from you. For example, you can install of virus-checking program, and you can set up that program to automatically check any file that you download from the internet. After you set up the program, you do not need to tell it to check a given file; it does so whenever it detects that you are downloading a file. Your subconscious computer works exactly the same way.

Think back to the time when you learned to ride a bicycle. Riding a bicycle is a very complex task, and at first most people find it difficult to prevent the bicycle from falling over. While trying to hold the balance, you also have to worry about your surroundings so that you do not end up in the ditch or get hit by a car. Riding a bicycle involves so many tasks that it quickly overwhelms your conscious mind. At first, it might seem impossible. However, after having practiced for while, most people suddenly "get it," and from then it becomes easy. After you learn how to keep the bicycle balanced, you no longer have to consciously worry about this task. Your attention is set free, and you can pretty much let your subconscious mind ride the bicycle while your conscious mind enjoys the scenery or decides where to go.

As you learn how to ride a bicycle, you are creating a computer program in your subconscious mind. This program quickly incorporates the mechanical aspects of riding a bicycle, from keeping it balanced to watching out for potential dangers. After the program has been created in your subconscious mind, it is constantly lying dormant, just as a computer program resides in the computer until it is activated. Whenever you get on a bicycle, your bicycle-riding program is activated. Many adults have gone for years or decades without riding a bicycle. Yet as soon as they get on a bicycle, the subconscious program kicks in and they can ride the bicycle without having to relearn the process.

Many of the daily tasks you perform are repetitive and many of them are very complex. If you were to perform them with your conscious mind, making choices at every stage, your mind would quickly become overwhelmed or bored. Why should you have to worry about riding a bicycle or performing many of the other routine tasks that you perform every day? By allowing a computer program in your subconscious mind to take over these tasks, you free up your conscious mind to do more enjoyable things.

Don't let a servant rule your life

The subconscious computer is a useful servant. However, why allow a servant to run your life. Unfortunately, that is what happens to most people.

If you perform a task or experience a situation more than once, your subconscious mind automatically begins to create a computer program aimed at performing the task or responding to the situation. These programs are not limited to mechanical tasks, such as riding a bicycle or brushing your teeth. You can create subconscious computer programs to deal with almost any conceivable situation. Therefore, throughout your life, you keep building subconscious programs for dealing with the types of situations you encounter.

Let us look at a relatively innocent example of how this can affect your life. Most young children love to draw, and they also love to receive praise for everything they do. Imagine a child who spends a long time making a drawing and then shows it to an adult. The adult invariably asks, "What is that?" The child might answer, "It's a house!" And the adult might say, "That doesn't look like a house!" or give the child some other type of negative feedback. Because of such adult reactions, many children create a subconscious computer program which states, "I can't draw!" After such computer programs are created, they affect people for the rest of their lives.

If you try to encourage adults to express themselves by drawing, many of them will say, "Oh, but I can't draw!" Yet these people may not have tried to draw for twenty years or more. If they haven't tried it for two decades, how do they know they can't draw? In reality, they don't know, and they are not making a conscious decision about the matter. They are allowing a subconscious computer program, created in childhood, to make the decision for them, and that decision limits their own creative expression.

Maintaining the subconscious computer

The belief that you cannot draw is a relatively harmless subconscious computer program. However, virtually any recurring situation from your childhood created a subconscious program, and many of these programs affect your basic world view, your attitude towards yourself and life, and your emotional reactions to certain situations. In recent decades, many psychologists have begun to realize just how much human beings can be the slaves of their subconscious minds. This has become especially clear in the cases of people who were sexually, physically or emotionally abused during childhood. They carry severe trauma with them for the rest of their lives, and it can affect everything they do.

If you are not consciously aware of how the subconscious computer affects your life, then you are likely to become a slave of that part of your mind. In reality, your subconscious mind should be your humble and obedient servant.

If you are serious about making progress on the spiritual path, you would benefit by taking control over your inner circumstance. To take control over your inner circumstance, you must take control over the subconscious computer. This task is not nearly as difficult as it might seem. If you are familiar with computers, you know that every now and then your computer's hard drive becomes too cluttered with files and programs that you no longer need. Therefore, you simply do a little house cleaning. Likewise, you also need to perform periodic maintenance of your subconscious computer.

The strong man syndrome

Unfortunately, many people seem to think that this is a very strange task, and they are reluctant to even take a look at their own psychology. This is especially the case for men who have grown up in a scientific and materialistic society. These men seem to think that dealing with their own psychology is some kind of "touchy-feely nonsense" that is beneath them. Yet this is mainly because they were not brought up with an understanding of how the human psyche affects every aspect of their lives.

Imagine that a nine-year-old boy is given a pair of new pants. He likes these pants so much that he wants to wear them all the time, and his mother has a hard time getting them washed. Now go forward ten years and imagine that the boy has turned into a young man. This young man still loves his pants so much that he insists on squeezing into them even at his present age. The pants no longer fit, but he just can't let go of these wonderful pants.

If you encountered such a person in real life, you would think that he was acting in a very strange manner. Yet most adults are still carrying around the subconscious computer programs that they developed in childhood. In many cases, people become so attached to these programs that they refuse to admit that they no longer serve a constructive purpose. This explains why some adults respond to certain situations with the emotional maturity of a child.

Incidentally, one might wonder why a sophisticated, scientifically minded society does not teach children how to take command of their own psyche. After all, the powers of this world find it necessary to teach all children about math, physics, biology and mechanical devices, such as computers. Why not teach children about the one factor that affects everything they do in life, namely the human psyche?

The question for you is, Do you want to spend the rest of your life being limited by subconscious computer programs that you no longer need? Or are you willing to do a little spring cleaning in the dark dungeons of your subconscious mind? If the answer to the latter question is yes, then you can take a major leap forward on your personal path. After an initial effort, you will be amazed at how your life will change for the better and how some of your problems will start to evaporate.

How to maintain the subconscious computer

Let us compare the process of healing your psychology to computer maintenance. As the computer industry matures, software companies come out with new and more advanced versions of their software. When you buy a new version of a software package, you need to remove the old version. If you do not, the old version might conflict with the new version and cause your computer to crash or to behave strangely.

Imagine that you encounter a very difficult situation at the age of nine and that your subconscious mind develops a program designed to help you deal with that situation. This program was a product of the understanding and maturity you had as a nine-year-old. You are now an adult, and you have grown in both maturity and understanding. If you were to encounter the original situation with your present level of maturity and understanding, you could handle that situation in a much better way than you did at the age of nine. However, because the old computer program still resides in your subconscious mind, you might still be responding to specific situations as you did when that program was first created. In other words, you could be responding to some situations with the emotional maturity of a nine-year-old even though you are now well into adulthood.

Conflicting subconscious computer programs

This reveals one of the most essential keys to personal growth. You need to develop a more mature version of the subconscious programs that help you deal with specific situations or that affect the way you look at yourself and your abilities. This involves removing the old program so that you do not have conflicting programs in your subconscious computer.

If you have too many programs installed on your computer, you increase the risk of a conflict between programs. This can cause your computer to crash or freeze, or it can cause it to behave in erratic or unpredictable ways. Likewise, if you have too many programs installed on your subconscious computer, some of those programs might work against each other. Do you ever encounter situations where you do not know what to do? Do you ever find it difficult to make a firm decision about how to handle a specific situation? If so, your indecision is probably a direct product of conflicting programs in your subconscious computer. Such conflicting programs can cause a warring in your members or a soul division, and this is why some people behave in erratic or irrational ways.

We earlier talked about one of the eternal questions of human existence, namely, why so many people do the things that they really do not want to do. We can now see that the reason for this behavior is the existence of one or more subconscious programs that override people's conscious minds. If these programs are strong, the conscious mind and willpower cannot override them. In reality, you are not in control of your life, because your reactions to a lot of situations are determined by subconscious programming. When you encounter a given situation, the subconscious program that was developed to handle those kind of situations automatically kicks in and takes over your thoughts, feelings and actions. The conscious self is simply standing by watching while another part of your mind has taken over the situation.

Are subconscious programs overpowering your free will?

The real problem with the subconscious programs is that they undermine your free will. If you allow subconscious programs to determine how you react to a specific situation, then you are not making a conscious choice about how you want to react to that situation. Obviously, this makes it impossible for you to take control over your inner circumstance, and therefore it is more difficult for you to make progress on your personal path.

We have already seen that the key to taking command of your inner circumstance is to bring your choices into the conscious mind. To make conscious choices, you must remove the subconscious computer programs that take over your responses to certain situations. In fact, some of these programs are constantly working, and they might determine how you look at yourself, how you look at life and how you relate to other people or to your higher self.

Many people have subconscious programs that are constantly sending negative messages into their conscious minds. For example, many people believe that they are sinners or that they have made such severe mistakes that they could never be forgiven and therefore be free of those mistakes. Other people experience that their subconscious minds are constantly telling them that they are no good at specific tasks or that they can never achieve certain goals. Many people have desires or goals, but every time they are about to achieve their goals, something happens that prevents their dreams from coming true. In most cases, this is caused by subconscious computer programs that cause them to sabotage their own efforts. When you consider the devastating effects these programs can have on your life, you can clearly see the need to clean out the hard drive in your subconscious computer.

Subconscious programs and your spiritual defense

The subconscious computer programs can sabotage your efforts to build a spiritual defense, and you need to understand how this can happen. Free will is one of the most fundamental laws of this universe. As we will see later, God did not want to create a race of mechanical robots. Therefore, God gave human beings the ability to choose freely. Neither God nor any of God's emissaries, including your higher self, will ever do anything to violate your free will. This has profound implications for your personal path.

Imagine that a girl grew up with a father who had a tendency towards anger and who directed that anger at her. As most children do, the little girl felt responsible for her father's anger, thinking that she somehow caused him to be angry. In reality, the father probably had a program in his subconscious mind that caused him to respond with anger to many of life's situations. Because the little girl did not know this, she developed her own computer program that caused her to respond to her father's anger with guilt and a false sense of responsibility. The girl has now grown into adulthood but has never made an effort to remove the subconscious program developed in childhood, and therefore she still responds to her father's anger with a sense of guilt and responsibility. In fact, she responds in a similar manner to any other authority figure, including God.

Now imagine that this woman reads these discourses and starts using spiritual techniques to build a shield of spiritual energy around her personal energy field. This shield can serve as a barrier against the toxic energies produced by her father's anger. Yet if the woman responds with guilt and a sense of responsibility, this reaction will neutralize the effects of her spiritual defense. Because of her own freewill choice, she will set aside the spiritual defense when it comes to her father's anger, and therefore the toxic energies produced by that anger can still enter her energy field. This does not mean that the woman's spiritual defenses are completely ineffective. They will still work in many other situations. However, to complete her spiritual defense, she needs to remove the subconscious computer program that causes a breach in her defense.

Stop the accident

One of the most important rules of first aid is to stop the accident and prevent the situation from getting worse. Earlier we saw that one of the keys to an effective spiritual defense is to invoke spiritual light, which transforms the toxic energies that are already stored in your energy field. But to take full advantage of this opportunity, you need to not only remove the energy that is already in your field. You also need to prevent yourself from generating more toxic energy inside your own mind. What causes you to produce such toxic energies?

These discourses have painted an image of a stream of spiritual energy that is constantly flowing from your higher self into your soul, or lower self. When the spiritual energies enter your lower self, they are pure, meaning that they are not qualified by any human thoughts or emotions. As the energies filter through the layers of your mind, these energies become qualified by your thoughts and feelings. As a result, they may be lowered in vibration until they fall below a certain threshold and become toxic energies.

What causes the misqualification of spiritual energy? At this point, it should be easy to see that your inner circumstance, meaning your subconscious programs, causes you to lower the vibration of spiritual energy until the energy becomes toxic. Any subconscious program that causes you to react with a negative feeling, such as fear or anger, will produce toxic energy. Some of this energy will be stored in your personal energy field.

Imagine that you apply the understanding you were given in the previous discourse and make a sincere effort to transform the negative energy that is already stored in your field. This approach will work, and you will lighten your load and reduce the amount of toxic energy in your field. However, if you continue to generate more toxic energy, then you will obviously not make progress as swiftly as possible. Why remove seventy-five "units" of toxic energy only to produce another fifty units in the same amount of time?

Instead, you need to attack the problem on both fronts. To efficiently free yourself from the effects of toxic energy, you need to do more than transform the existing toxic energy. You must also engage in a process of removing the subconscious programs that produce more toxic energy. By applying this one-two punch, you can make much swifter progress on the path.

Why prayer isn't always answered

The idea that your freewill choices can neutralize your spiritual defense explains one of the questions that has baffled many spiritual and religious people throughout the ages. This question is, Why aren't prayers always answered?

The explanation is that neither God nor any spiritual being will violate your free will. Many people pray to God with their conscious minds, only to have their conscious prayer be counteracted by a subconscious computer program. If you have a warring in your members, a conflict in your psyche or division in your soul, then you are constantly sending mixed messages to God or to your higher self. Which one of these conflicting messages should God respond to?

You have been given the gift of free will, and it is your supreme personal responsibility to learn how to use that free will wisely. If you have a warring in your members, then you must make the conscious choice to change the situation. As long as the war continues, some of your prayers might not be answered. However, if you will make a sincere effort to resolve the conflict in your psyche, you will experience that God will begin to answer your prayers with a speed and power that most people consider impossible. "Prove me herewith says the Lord, and I shall pour out a blessing so that there will not be room enough to receive it."

Breaking your negative spirals

We have seen that many people find themselves in a negative, downward or self-destructive spiral and that they find it extremely difficult to break out of such a pattern. We can now see that breaking this pattern is not nearly as difficult as it might seem. Once you understand what causes the negative spiral, you can see what you can do to break it.

A negative spiral always starts with a subconscious program, which is created by repetition. For example, a child might experience verbal abuse over an extended period of time, and gradually the child builds a negative self-image. After a subconscious program is created, it causes you to misqualify spiritual energy so that it becomes toxic energy. Some of this energy is stored in your personal energy field, and as it reaches a critical mass it will create a gravitational pull that will start affecting your conscious thoughts and feelings.

When you encounter a situation that activates the subconscious program, your mind immediately comes under the gravitational pull of the toxic energy that was misqualified as a result of the program. That is why most people have certain situations from the past which cause them intense emotional pain many years later. Whenever you are reminded of the situation that created the emotional scar, your feelings immediately become affected by the gravitational pull of the toxic energy that is stored in your field. Therefore, you experience the emotional pain with virtually the same intensity that you felt in the original situation. In fact, the emotional pain might grow as more and more energy is stored in your field.

After the toxic energy reaches a critical mass and starts overpowering your conscious mind, the gravitational pull of the energy will reinforce the subconscious program. For example, if you have a subconscious program that causes you to respond to certain situations with anger, the toxic energies stored in your field will cause your anger to gradually become more intense. That is why, over a period of time, some people build up an intense anger which they cannot control. A similar process applies to any other negative feeling, and if this process is allowed to continue unchecked, people will eventually "lose it," as the popular saying goes.

Negative spirals prevent your growth

The combination of a subconscious program that is being reinforced by an intense gravitational pull of toxic energy can easily overwhelm your conscious mind and your conscious willpower. Obviously, this can have a number of negative effects on your daily life. However, it can also affect your ability to heal your emotional wounds. When people seek to heal themselves, through self-help efforts or various forms of therapy, they often encounter the following situation.

Because people did not grow up with an understanding of the human psyche and of the need to heal their emotional wounds from the past, they generally tend to cover over and ignore those wounds as long as possible. People try to get by until they experience some kind of crisis through which they finally realize that they have to do something about their psychology. Unfortunately, while they ignored the problem, the subconscious program caused them to build up a large reservoir of toxic energy in their personal energy fields.

When a person finally recognizes the problem and goes into therapy in an attempt to heal the problem, that person invariably taps into this reservoir of toxic energy. The intensity of the toxic energy causes some people to become so scared that they immediately pull out of therapy. They go into a state of denial, nevermore to acknowledge the problem or the need for healing. Other people become so overwhelmed by the energy that the positive effects of their therapy are neutralized. In fact, many people have spent years in therapy without making significant progress towards resolving the original problem because the intensity of the energy makes it impossible for them to get to the root of the problem. People are dealing with the energy effects without ever uncovering the subconscious programming that is the cause of their emotional scars. Every year people waste millions of dollars and thousands of hours on therapy that never gets past the effects, namely the toxic energy stored in their energy fields.

If you are willing to apply the inner approach to knowledge, it will become easy to see how to break such a negative spiral:

- Begin by applying an effective technique for transforming the toxic energy that is stored in your energy field. If you know that you have a specific problem or a specific emotional scar from childhood, then be very specific and direct high-frequency spiritual energy into the toxic energy that was produced by that emotional scar.

- Uncover and dissolve the subconscious programming that started the negative spiral in the first place. You need to heal that emotional wound and take back your ability to freely choose how you will respond to a given situation.

Dissolving a subconscious program

How do you remove an obsolete or limiting program from your subconscious computer? The key is to realize that every subconscious program started with a choice, and that choice was made by you.

For many people, this idea can seem very harsh and some refuse to accept it. If all of your personal limitations originated with a choice that you made, then everything in your life becomes your own responsibility. Therefore, it often seems easier to reject personal responsibility, and while this emotional reaction is understandable, it is not very constructive. If you deny that your inner circumstance is the product of your own choices, then you also give away your power to change your circumstance.

By accepting responsibility for your inner circumstance, you open up vast new opportunities for taking command of your life. The wonderful thing about choices is that they are so easy to make. The way to undo a wrong or bad choice is to make a better choice.

Imagine that you encountered a traumatic situation at the age of five. Your reaction to that situation was a result of the understanding and the emotional maturity you had at that age. Therefore, the choice that started the subconscious programming was the choice of a five-year-old. That choice is not set in stone. You can undo that choice at any time by replacing it with a better choice, a choice that reflects your present understanding and maturity. If you base your new choice on right understanding from your higher self, then you can create a new program that will replace the original program. Your new program will reflect your present understanding and maturity. Therefore it will not limit you, but it will empower you.

The key to dissolving the subconscious programs that were created in the past is to mentally go back to the situation in which the program started. When you understand the choice that created the program, you can replace the original choice with a better choice. If you are willing to apply the inner approach to knowledge, then your higher self will take you by the hand and lead you to situations in your past where you need to make a better and more mature choice. This process will require some effort on your part, and it might cause you to experience the emotional pain of the original situation. However, if you will apply an efficient technique for transforming the toxic energy created by the program, the emotional pain will be greatly reduced and you will experience only a slight discomfort. The reward for enjoying this mental flashback to a painful past is that you can permanently free yourself from the negative effects of that past. So the question really becomes, Do you want the rest of your life to be dominated by a painful situation from your past, or do you want to temporarily go back to that situation so that you can permanently free yourself from its negative effects?

It should be obvious that the effort required to remove your subconscious computer programs represents a very small investment that can pay huge dividends in the form of greater peace of mind and greater enjoyment of life. If you have read these discourses up to this point, then you are ready to engage in this process. You need to consciously acknowledge that you are willing to make the effort to transcend your past.

How to transcend your past

Let us look at practical ways whereby you can free yourself from of your past. The essential key to this process is the inner approach to knowledge whereby you contact your higher self. Your higher self can and will give you the direction you need if you will listen with an open mind. However, you can greatly speed up this process by taking certain outer steps to help you discover the specific subconscious programs that you need to overcome. This process has the following elements:

Awareness

You need to become aware that you have a certain problem in your life and develop a motivation to do something about that problem. Perhaps you are already painfully aware of a particular problem and perhaps you have already developed plenty of motivation. If not, you need to do some soul-searching to find out which aspects of your life are limiting your sense of enjoyment and peace of mind.

Do you have certain goals that you cannot seem to fulfill? Do you have certain problems that you experience over and over again? Do you encounter certain situations that always result in a painful emotional reaction? To help you go through this process, it can be valuable to gain a greater understanding of the human psyche. Numerous books can help you do this, and most can be found in categories such as motivational literature, psychology and self-improvement, inspirational or New Age. You may want to visit a large bookstore or library and look through these categories. Select one or two books that speak to your heart and then start reading. If you complete one book without having a clear understanding of what you need to work on, then move on to another. If you will apply the inner approach to knowledge as you read the books, you will soon discover some of the things that are holding you back. See the bibliography for specific suggestions of what to read.

Understanding
You need to develop an understanding of the psychological mechanisms that cause certain outer conditions. For example, you might have low self-esteem which prevents you from fulfilling your dreams. What caused you to develop a negative self-image?

Once again, it can be invaluable to read books on psychology. Start by developing a general understanding of psychology. After you develop this general knowledge, you will find it easy to go into specific areas that relate to your personal situation. If you encountered particular problems in childhood, you can probably find a book that addresses those problems.

You might think, "Why can't I get the understanding I need from my higher self?" The answer is that your higher self needs a way to communicate that understanding to your outer mind, and it can only do so if you have some knowledge about the problem you are working on. If you know nothing about psychology, then your higher self does not have any concepts to work with. Remember that your higher self does not make choices for you. You make choices through your conscious mind, using your free will. So to make right choices, you need conscious understanding. You get this understanding by expanding your outer knowledge of psychology and at the same time listening for an understanding that comes from within.

Application
Find a technique that allows you to mentally step back into the past and experience the creation of a specific subconscious program. Discourse 6 will present one such technique but you can find many more. You can find some of these

techniques in books on psychology, self-help and self-improvement.

By applying the inner approach to knowledge as you read these books, you can gain significant results. However, you can greatly speed up the healing process by taking advantage of various forms of therapy. To effectively heal your psychology, it can be invaluable to have the help of another person who can walk you through the different steps without being emotionally involved with your situation. If you know that you have suffered severe abuse in childhood, you should not attempt to tackle the situation on your own. Instead, find an experienced professional who can help you go through the process of healing.

Steps to healing

Whatever methods you decide to employ, whether you choose to read books or engage in various forms of therapy, always apply the following steps:

- Remember that the foundation for the healing process is to take the inner approach to knowledge. Therefore, always base your efforts on right understanding, which comes primarily from your higher self. Use any outer sources, such as books or therapists, as a way to stimulate the process of getting answers from within.

- Find and apply an effective spiritual technique that allows you to build a strong spiritual defense. Be especially conscious of the need to transform the toxic energies that are stored in your personal energy field so that you can remove their gravitational pull on your conscious mind.

- Always remember that the goal of your healing effort is to uncover your subconscious programming and to dissolve it by making a better choice based on right understanding.

- Do not allow yourself to become discouraged and do not expect too much. Your subconscious programs have been built up over a long period of time, and they will not all be dissolved in a day or two. Therefore, start slowly and expect that the process will take time.

- Expect that it will take time for you to become familiar with the process of healing. Many people anticipate immediate results and give up when the results do not appear that quickly. You will get better results from taking a more gradual approach and slowly building your confidence in the process.

- Start out with a relatively small problem and resolve that one first. Then, as you gain more confidence in the process, start attacking some of the bigger problems.

- If you encounter a problem that seems overwhelming, seek to break that problem into smaller units. Then, attack the smaller problems one at a time. Always remember that the only way to complete a journey of a thousand miles is to take one small step at a time.

The key to success

Perhaps you feel hesitant or afraid about this journey into the uncharted waters of your subconscious mind. Remind yourself that the key to all progress is the magic word—try.

Making Truly Free Choices

Make a conscious choice to give it a try, and make a commitment to apply a specific approach for at least six months. Then, evaluate the results and make a decision about how you will continue. If you apply the inner approach throughout the process, you will be amazed at the results. Lifelong problems and burdens will gradually start to dissolve. After a certain amount of time (which varies from person to person), you will break through and realize that you have reached an entirely new level of empowerment and peace of mind.

Keep in mind that the journey has many stages. Here are just a few of the things you can expect (though they might not happen in this order):

- You will see the resolution of a particular problem or crisis.

- You will start to notice that you no longer seem to run into specific situations or problems.

- You will suddenly realize that you no longer feel the emotional pain of certain situations from the past.

- You will start realizing that your life no longer goes from one crisis to the next but that you have achieved (and earned) the freedom to pursue your positive goals.

- Your relationships will begin to change in profound ways. As you become more positive, you will no longer encounter as many negative people and you will start attracting more positive people.

- You will begin to feel a growth in self-confidence, and you will build a positive image of yourself and life.

- As you experience more and more positive results, you will begin to accept that this path has no glass ceiling.

- You will begin to develop happiness and peace of mind.

- You will greatly increase your understanding of your true, inner identity.

- You will find answers to some of your questions about life and your personal situation.

- You will begin to develop an entirely new relationship to your higher self, and thereby you will develop a new relationship with God.

As you experience these results, you will eventually begin to understand that what might have started out as a desperate attempt to escape a particular crisis has now turned into an exciting and enjoyable journey of self-discovery.

DISCOURSE 6:
Your Action Plan for Personal Growth

These discourses are meant to give you tools for overcoming the obstacles that obstruct your progress on the path. We now need to look at an obstacle that prevents many people from getting practical results from their self-help efforts. Some people read several self-help books, and they acquire a great intellectual understanding of psychology and personal growth. Yet they do not experience significant results from their efforts, and the reason is that they don't translate their knowledge into action.

We have seen that self-help efforts must be based on right understanding; however, right understanding is only one side of the coin. To change your life, you need to let the inner understanding be reflected in your outer actions. Unfortunately, many people falter on the doorstep to a new life because they do not translate their knowledge into action. What does it take to get past this hurdle? You need to make a decision with your conscious mind!

The engine of your personal growth is the inner understanding you get from your higher self. Compare this to the engine of a car and take note that the engine alone cannot get the car to its destination. For the car to reach its goal, someone must put the car in gear and steer the car in the right direction. For you to reach your destination, someone must be in the driver's seat, and that someone is your conscious mind. We have already discussed that some people are not willing to take an active approach to life but would rather be driven by the wind and tossed. If you are serious about the path, it helps to be aware that the path is not a matter of reading a book, accepting a certain doctrine or practicing a self-help technique. You cannot make it on autopilot. The path is not a mechanical but an artistic process. The path is not a matter of pushing the right buttons but making the right choices.

You are a unique individual. Your personal path is not predetermined by forces outside your control. Your path is a work of art, and only you can choose the right colors and the right brush strokes. Through this book, you can find many of the essential tools you need to turn your life into a positive, upward spiral. If you have read this far, your spiritual engine has already been started. However, the catalyst for positive change will be putting the car in gear and accepting that it is up to you to steer yourself in the right direction.

Your higher self can give you tremendous assistance on the path by providing understanding. However, your higher self will not make choices for you. Therefore, you must take the first step, and you must continue to take one small step at a time until you have completed the journey. Your path might not be a journey of a thousand miles; nevertheless it will not be completed overnight. You need to get started, and then decide to keep going until you see results.

The main reason that some people don't translate their understanding into action is that they don't realize that the master key to personal growth is to make better choices. They are paralyzed in a situation that is similar to the one faced by Hamlet when he uttered the famous question, "To be or not to be?"

How do you get started? You can begin by experimenting with the tools you have received in this book. You might begin by creating a personal action plan that contains the following elements:

- Seek to improve your intuition and expand your conscious contact to your higher self.

- Protect yourself from toxic energy. You need to remove the energy that is already stored in your personal energy field, seal yourself from external energy and stop producing toxic energy internally.

- Seek to identify and replace the negative programming in your subconscious mind. This includes overcoming incomplete, incorrect or self-defeating beliefs.

The following sections will suggest several techniques that will help you accomplish these tasks. You can use these techniques to develop a personal action plan that defines what you will do and how often you will do it. For the best possible start, make a commitment that you will apply this plan for at least six months. Then, evaluate your progress and adjust your action plan according to your inner direction. If you make a sincere effort, you will be receptive to such inner direction!

Sealing yourself from toxic energy
To seal yourself from toxic energy, do the following:

1. Go into a quiet room, a room in which you can remain undisturbed for 5-10 minutes or for as long as you want.

2. Sit in a comfortable chair with your arms and legs uncrossed. Find a comfortable position that you can maintain without being distracted by discomfort in your body. If it feels better to lie down, do so.

3. Close your eyes and use a relaxation technique to relax your body and mind. For example, tighten the muscles in one part of your body and hold them tight for a few seconds before relaxing them. Do the same for every part of your body. As an alternative, you can listen to soothing music, such as the Pachelbel Canon.

4. When you feel relaxed, visualize your higher self as being somewhere above your head. Visualize that your higher self lowers a wall of white light around your body and your personal energy field. The wall is several feet thick, and it completely surrounds your energy field. This light forms a shield of high-frequency energy around your energy field. The energy vibrates so quickly that none of the energies from the material octave could possibly penetrate it. Such lower energies would bounce off the wall of light.

5. Take some time to fully immerse yourself in this visualization. Feel that the wall of white light is very real and tangible, almost physical. Allow yourself to feel like you are sealed from any disturbing or inharmonious energies from the outside world. Absolutely nothing can touch you inside that wall of light, as if you are in another dimension or octave.

6. When you truly experience the wall of light, visualize that your higher self lights a spiritual fire under your feet. This fire is composed of violet light of an intense, almost electric, appearance. The fire burns from a place under your feet, but the flames envelop your body and your energy field, filling the space inside the wall of white light.

7. The violet fire has the power to transmute negative energies stored in your personal field. These energies tend to gravitate to the lower half of your field. You can visualize the energy field as an egg-shaped area around your body. The lower part of the egg forms a bowl that stores toxic energies. Visualize a concentrated violet flame burning in the lower part of your field and consuming all toxic energies.

8. If you have a specific situation that causes you pain, allow yourself to feel the energies from that situation. Then, visualize an intense violet flame enveloping the situation and consuming the toxic energies. You can also visualize your higher self sending a beam of concentrated violet light into the situation or into the energies in your field.

9. If you feel you need extra protection, visualize a wall of electric blue light surrounding the wall of white light.

Practice this visualization every morning and evening. As you practice, the wall of light may start to appear automatically whenever you turn your attention towards your higher self. The goal of this exercise is to become so familiar with the wall of light that you can visualize it in any situation. Whenever you encounter a situation in which you feel negative energy, visualize the wall of light around you and accept that you are sealed from all toxic energies.

At first, this exercise might seem a bit strange. However, if you make a sincere effort, you will quickly become familiar with the idea of spiritual protection. The power of your wall of light is in direct proportion to your power of visualization and your belief that this actually works. Contemplate the words of Henry Ford, "Whether you believe you can, or whether you believe you can't—you're right!" If you believe that the wall of light seals you from toxic energies, you will soon begin to experience that it actually works. As a result, you will start to feel more calm in stressful situations.

Sending light into specific situations

When you feel comfortable with the wall of light visualization, you can build upon it. Go through the steps to establish your wall of light. When you feel enveloped by the white wall and the violet fire, visualize your higher self sending a concentrated beam of spiritual light into a specific situation. Let the color of the light depend on the situation, and use the colors described in a previous discourse. For example, you might visualize golden light enveloping yourself, another person or a situation and consuming all negative energy that blocks a deeper understanding. You might visualize emerald green light enveloping a particular illness and consuming all toxic energy that contributes to the condition.

When your visualization involves other people, always remember to maintain ultimate respect for their free will. In other words, you wouldn't want to force or manipulate other people to act in a certain way. Instead, visualize them protected by blue light, healed by green light or illumined by golden light so that they can make the best possible choices.

Always qualify your visualization according to the vision of your higher self or a spiritual figure. For example, you might mentally say:

In accordance with the perfect vision of my higher self, I invoke light into (briefly describe the situation).

If you are a Christian, you might say:

In the name of Jesus Christ and in accordance with the will of God, I invoke light into (briefly describe the situation).

You can make similar affirmations using the names of other religious figures.

Getting answers from within

The following visualization is designed to help you get answers from inside yourself. This can be an understanding of yourself or any situation you face. You can also use this visualization to select a spiritual technique. The technique is designed specifically to help you gain direct contact with your higher self.

1. Start by performing the visualization of the wall of light and the violet flame. When you feel fully enveloped in the wall of light, move to the next step.

2. Focus your attention on the center of your chest, at the height of your heart. Visualize a spiritual flame burning in the center of your chest. It is an unfed flame, meaning that it burns without fuel.

3. Visualize your soul walking into this spiritual flame. A doorway, portal or tunnel opens up. This passageway leads into another octave, a world in which everything is light.

4. As you come through the passage, you find yourself in a beautiful garden. The garden is surrounded by walls that are covered with flowering vines, and it has flower beds with numerous beautiful flowers that

fill the air with their fragrance. In the distance, birds are singing.

5. As you walk into the garden, you come upon two seats that are facing each other. You sit down in one seat, and your spiritual teacher is sitting in the other seat, facing you. You can visualize the teacher as your higher self or as a particular religious figure, such as Jesus, Buddha or another spiritual master. If you choose to visualize your higher self, you might see it in a human form that radiates an intense white light.

6. Give yourself a minute to feel completely at peace in this tranquil garden. Allow yourself to feel the radiation of your spiritual teacher. Your spiritual teacher has no judgment towards you or anything you have ever done. Your teacher radiates unconditional and infinite love for your soul. Allow yourself to feel that love.

7. When you feel enveloped in the love of your teacher, briefly direct your attention towards a problem, question or situation for which you want to receive a deeper understanding. Present the situation to your teacher, either in words or images. Then, ask your teacher for understanding. For example, you might say, "Please give me a deeper understanding of this situation."

8. After you make your request, allow yourself to let go of the situation or problem. Focus your attention on the spiritual teacher or the beautiful garden. Allow yourself to be absorbed in the peace, tranquility and love of your surroundings.

9. After a while, your attention might naturally return to your request or to the situation you were concerned about. When that happens, listen for a response coming from inside your heart. If you do not get an immediate answer, be not disturbed. Simply reason that you will get the response later.

10. Spend as much time as you like in the beautiful garden, absorbing the spiritual light of your teacher. When you are ready to return to your normal state of consciousness, visualize yourself leaving the garden and walking through the passageway.

11. As you emerge from the passageway, you are surrounded by the wall of light. Gently return to your normal state of consciousness.

In the beginning, you might not get an immediate response to your request. The answer might come sometime later. Depending on the nature of the request, it might take hours, days or even weeks. Do not despair. Simply allow the process to take its time, and repeat the exercise as many times as you feel is necessary.

The essential key to getting clear and accurate responses from your higher self is to realize that your higher self is not your personal psychic hotline. Your higher self and genuine spiritual teachers will not violate your free will or make choices for you. The role of a spiritual teacher is to help you gain a true understanding of a situation so that you have the best possible foundation for making right choices with your conscious mind. Therefore, a true spiritual teacher will not tell you what to do or how to do it. So, do not ask, "What should I do about this situation?" Instead, ask, "What is a better way to look at this situation; what is a deeper understanding of the situation?"

If you will follow this simple rule and practice the exercise, you will be amazed at the results you can achieve. However, remember that it is your job to make conscious choices. Do not attempt to have your higher self or spiritual teacher tell you everything about every situation. A spiritual teacher will not seek to make you codependent. The goal of a spiritual teacher is to help you make choices on your own.

Establishing a contact with your higher self is an essential part of the path. If you feel the need for additional information, you can find some excellent books on developing intuition. For more information, see the bibliography.

The flow of light

The following exercise is designed to help you establish a constant stream of spiritual light flowing from your higher self into your personal energy field and back to your higher self. One of the main problems with any kind of visualization or spiritual exercise is that your thoughts can easily get distracted. The following exercise is designed to minimize distraction from your outer mind. It is also designed to help the two halves of your brain come into harmony and coherence. In preparation, do the following:

1. Sit in a comfortable chair and invoke the wall of light.

2. Visualize yourself standing inside the wall of light. Your higher self is located approximately six feet above your head (see the following illustration).

3. Visualize the figure of the number eight superimposed over your higher self and your body. The nexus of the figure eight is over the center of your chest at the level of your heart. The upper part of the figure

Your Action Plan for Personal Growth 127

eight goes through your higher self. The lower part of the figure eight goes through the lower part of your energy field.

Use the chart to visualize the flow of light. The numbers on the chart correspond to the steps below:

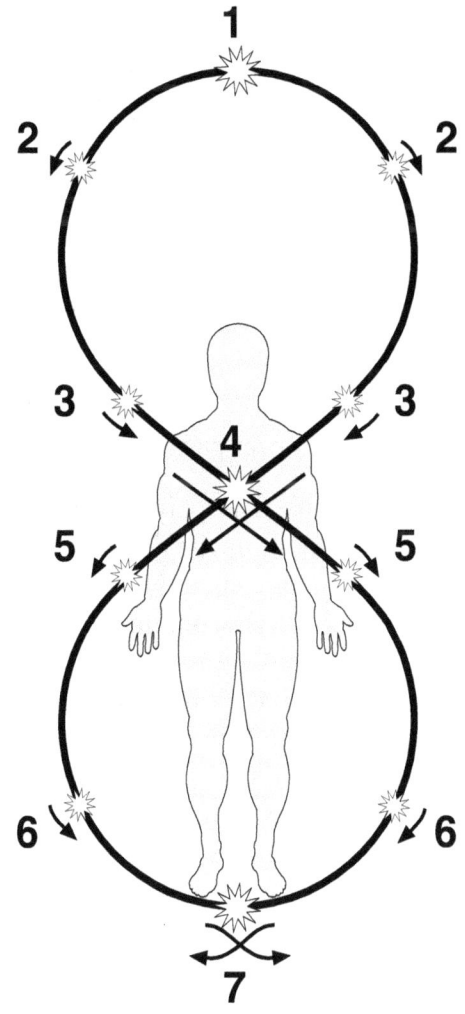

1. Visualize a point of light over your higher self.

2. The point of light splits into two points that start moving down the sides of the upper half of the figure eight.

3. The points keep moving towards the nexus of the figure.

4. The points reach the nexus at exactly the same time. They move through the nexus, crossing each other.

5. The points move down the lower half of the figure.

6. The points move towards the lowest point of the figure.

7. The two points reach the bottom of the figure at the exact same time. Then they cross each other and start moving up the lower part of the figure eight.

Reverse the above steps. The points of light move to the nexus, cross over and move up the upper part until they meet again at the top of the figure eight. Now repeat the steps. Visualize the two points of light continuously moving through the figure eight.

In the beginning, you don't need to worry about visualizing a perfect figure eight. However, the two points of light should reach each of the three crossover points at the exact same time. As you become more experienced with this exercise, work on visualizing a perfect figure eight.

Practice this exercise for as long as it feels comfortable, perhaps only a few minutes, perhaps five or ten minutes. Allow yourself to become absorbed in the continuous flow of the two points of light. Repeat the exercise each morning and evening. When you feel comfortable performing this exercise, you can build upon it as described below.

Bringing light into your energy field

When you are completely comfortable with the exercise and able to visualize the flow of the two points of light, use the following visualization:

1. Go through the exercise of visualizing the two points of light flowing through the figure eight.

2. When the two points of light reach the bottom of your figure eight (the bottom of your personal energy field), visualize that they release an intense spark of light that radiates into the lower part of your field.

3. The two points of light also attract some of the negative energy that is stored in the lower part of your field. The points of light carry this negative energy up to your higher self where it is consumed by the spiritual fire or your higher self. In other words, you are now visualizing that the figure-eight flow brings spiritual light into your energy field and draws some of the imperfect energy back to your spiritual self. You are, literally, receiving perfect light from your higher self and giving imperfect light back to your higher self, where it is transformed back into perfect light.

4. As you go through this exercise, visualize that the lower part of your personal energy field gradually fills up with spiritual light. This spiritual light fills the vacuum that is created by the imperfect energy that is sent back up to your higher self.

When you feel comfortable with this new visualization, you can visualize that the figure-eight flow envelops specific situations. Once again, the two points of light bring spiritual light down from your higher self and this light envelops the entire situation. The two points of light also carry imperfect energy back up to your higher self.

Being in your higher self

When you feel completely comfortable with the flow of light from your higher self through the figure eight, move on to the following visualization:

1. Before you start the flow of light, focus your attention in the center of your chest at the level of your heart.

2. Visualize a spiritual flame and see that your soul enters that flame.

3. Behind the flame is a tunnel that leads straight up to your higher self, which is located six feet above your head. Allow yourself to feel that you are now seated in your higher self, looking down upon your body and your personal energy field.

4. Now start the two points of light directly from your higher self.

5. See how they flow down through the figure eight and return back up.

In this exercise, you are not looking at your body or your higher self from an outside point of view. You are in your higher self, looking down at your body. As you become more familiar with this visualization, allow yourself to feel that your soul and sense of identity merge with your higher self. Feel that you are that higher self and visualize how the spiritual being that you are sends spiritual light into your personal energy field. This light fills your personal field and consumes all imperfect energies.

The power of the spoken word

Visualization is a very powerful technique for invoking spiritual light. However, you can achieve even better results by using the power of the spoken word. According to the Vedas, the oldest spiritual texts found on this planet, sound is the basic force used to create the entire universe. This has a parallel in the Bible, when God said, "Let there be light!"

The most powerful way to invoke spiritual light is to use the spoken word to affirm that spiritual light is manifest in your world. The most powerful affirmations begin with the words "I AM." Thereby, you affirm that you are the spiritual light in action in your world. If you are Christian, you will notice that Jesus used this technique on numerous occasions. Jesus used several I AM affirmations, such as, "I AM the resurrection and the life!" "I AM the light which lighteth every man that comes into the world" or "I AM the open door which no man can shut!"

An effective affirmation has the following elements:

- Start by giving a brief introduction to direct the light. For example, you might say, "In the name of my own higher self, I call forth spiritual light into... (briefly describe a situation in which you want to see positive change). A more effective introduction is, "In the name of the Living God, in the name of Jesus Christ (or your preferred religious figure), I invoke the light of God that never fails to consume all imperfect energies in... (briefly describe a situation)."

- After the introduction, give one or several affirmations. It is most effective to give each affirmation three times or in multiples of three, be it 9, 12 or 36 times.

- After the affirmations, give a sealing statement. For example, you might say, "I accept God's light and God's perfection manifest in my life. In accordance with God's will, it is done! Amen."

When you give affirmations, keep in mind that negative energy has formed over a period of time. Therefore, you need to repeat the affirmations many times in one session. You also need to give a set of affirmations every day for an extended period. For each time you repeat an affirmation, you peel off a layer of toxic energy. At some point, you reach a critical mass and you begin to notice results. Perhaps you suddenly realize that a painful situation from your past no longer has the power to disturb you. The reason is that the toxic energy no longer exerts a gravitational pull on your thoughts and feelings.

Affirmations

The following affirmations are designed for invoking spiritual light. As you give the affirmations, visualize that spiritual light envelops yourself, your energy field, another person, a specific situation or the world.

Let there be light, light, light!

I AM light, light, light!

I AM divine light consuming all darkness in my energy field! (Or in your body or in a specific situation.)

I AM the resurrection and the life!

I AM the resurrection and the life of my energy field! (Or your body or a specific situation.)

I AM a being of spiritual light!

I AM the light of God consuming all imperfections in my energy field! (Or your body or a specific situation).

I AM the light of God filling my entire energy field! (Or your body or a specific situation.)

The following affirmations are designed to invoke the assistance of your higher self or a religious figure that is dear to your heart. Instead of the words "higher self," you can insert the name of a religious figure, such as Jesus or Buddha.

Beloved Higher Self, I invite you into my temple, and I ask to be filled with your unconditional love.

I accept the unconditional love of my Higher Self, and I accept that I am worthy of that love.

I accept and affirm that my Higher Self is with me always.

I accept my freedom from all imperfections and pain of the past. My Higher Self delivers me now, and I am made whole.

Beloved Higher Self, I accept that you are setting me free from all imperfect beliefs.

Beloved Higher Self, I accept that you are delivering me from all imperfect energies.

Beloved Higher Self, I am willing to walk the path of personal growth. Show me the way.

Beloved Higher Self, I accept that you are consuming my subconscious programming, and I surrender it all to you.

(Instead of "subconscious programming," you can be more specific. For example, you can insert "fear and doubt" or "anger.")

Pick as many of these affirmations as you like. You can also make your own affirmations for specific situations. If you belong to a particular religious organization or group, you might find inspiration for such affirmations within its teachings.

Human beings have always had a need to transform toxic energy. Therefore, most religious or spiritual movements have developed techniques for this purpose. For example, many religions use the power of the spoken word in the form of various chants. Within the last century, several organizations have published techniques that use the spoken word to transform toxic energy. For a large selection of affirmations, see www.askrealjesus.com in the Personal Growth section.

Please keep in mind that these discourses are not meant to convert you to a particular belief system. You can easily use the techniques offered by an organization without becoming a member of that organization or accepting its belief system. Simply follow the direction of your higher self, but make sure you listen with an open mind.

Developing your personal plan

The key to getting off to a good start is to select a spiritual technique that helps you overcome toxic energy. You can use the technique for contacting your higher self to determine which technique is best for you. Then, make a commitment to practice that technique every day for ten to fifteen minutes or more. However, it is best not to set your goals too high, but make sure you can fit your chosen activities into your daily schedule. Set a realistic goal that you can keep instead of a lofty goal that you cannot meet in the long run.

After you start practicing a technique, set aside some time to go through the following steps. If you do not get results the first time, do not despair. Simply keep repeating the procedure until you get inner direction. Constancy and persistence are important elements of the spiritual path. It has taken time for you to build up a wall of negative energy around your conscious mind, and it may take time and effort to penetrate the density of this energy so that the light of your higher self can shine through the clouds that obstruct your vision.

Throughout this process, always have a notebook and pen ready so that you can write down any directions you get from within. You might find it helpful to keep a regular journal to preserve a record of your progress. Also, be ready to write down any questions or answers that come to you during the day.

Determining what to work on
The first step is to determine what you want to work on, and you can find out what it is by looking within. You have two possibilities:

- If you do not have a clear inner direction of what to work on, apply the technique for contacting your higher self. As you are seated in the garden, ask your higher self or spiritual teacher to help you understand what you need to work on right now. If you do not get a clear answer, it might help to read a book that will give you a greater understanding of general psychological issues. Apply the technique as you read the book.

- If you already have a clear inner direction, move on to the next step.

Gaining greater clarity
When you know what you want to work on, apply the technique for contacting your higher self for the purpose of gaining a greater understanding of the problem, situation or condition. Ask your higher self or spiritual teacher to help you understand the effects and the cause of the problem. Also, ask for help in understanding how to best resolve the problem.

If you do not get a clear answer or if you feel that you need an even deeper understanding, read a book that describes the problem. The more knowledge you have in your conscious awareness, the easier it is for your higher self to give you a greater understanding. The outer understanding gives your higher self a basis for communicating with your conscious mind. If you are dealing with a problem that brings up a lot of painful memories or emotional energy, try not to force a greater understanding. Instead, apply the next step and later try to expand your understanding of the problem.

Invoking light

When you have achieved some understanding of what you need to work on, apply a technique for invoking light and direct that light into all aspects of the problem. This can include specific outer situations, but it should focus on negative energy stored in your personal energy field.

Be specific and visualize spiritual light consuming all negative energy that relates to the problem or that was produced by a certain condition. Make up your personal affirmations and use them to consume negative energy relating to the problem. Also, affirm the positive outcome of the situation or problem. If your problem relates to negative behavior or emotions, create affirmations that affirm positive emotions or actions.

Keep invoking light until you feel that the emotional pain or intensity has been reduced to a manageable level. Then move on to the next step.

Going deeper

Use the technique for contacting your higher self, and seek to gain a deeper understanding of the problem. Once again, it might be helpful to read books on psychology or self-help. If you feel a need to take advantage of professional help, by all means do so at this stage. As you go deeper, you might uncover different aspects of the problem. Sometimes you might start working on one problem only to find that it was not the real issue. In many cases, a minor problem prevents you from seeing a larger, underlying problem. Therefore, you need to be flexible and follow your inner direction as you move to deeper layers of the subconscious mind. Whenever you reach a deeper layer, move on to the next step.

As you uncover a deeper level of the problem, you might run into a new pool of toxic energy that causes emotional pain. Once again, invoke light into that energy and consume it before you move on.

Identifying toxic decisions

For each layer that you uncover, seek to find a decision that caused you to accept any negative or limiting belief about yourself or your abilities. This can be something simple, such as, "I can't draw." Or it can be much more devastating, such as, "I am a bad person."

When you do identify a toxic decision, use the technique for contacting your higher self. While seated in front of your higher self and feeling its unconditional love, take a look at the situation in which you made the toxic decision. Allow yourself to relive the situation without becoming lost in it. Seek to understand why you made the original decision. Then, step back from the situation and calmly realize that the decision you made was a product of the understanding and maturity you had at the time.

Now, allow yourself to feel that you have gained a new understanding and a higher maturity. Therefore, visualize how you would handle the situation with the understanding and maturity you have now. Always seek the advice of your higher self to get the best possible understanding of the situation so that you can make the best possible decision.

Take your time and allow your new decision to come from within. If you seek to force a decision with your outer mind, you will not replace the original decision. Instead, you might create a new computer program that conflicts the original one. Instead of gaining true resolution, you only increase your subconscious conflicts. Take your time and seek to truly understand the situation. The basic idea is that when you fully understand the situation, you clearly see why the original decision was immature, incomplete or even wrong. This recognition, this inner clarity, will naturally bring about the new decision. If you truly know better, you will inevitably make a better decision! After you make a better decision, move on to the next step.

Solidifying your victory
When you have made a better decision, solidify that victory by doing the following:

• Invoke spiritual light and direct it into consuming all negative energy and emotional pain that was caused by that original decision. Keep doing this until you can think about the original decision without feeling emotional pain. You want to be able to look at that decision, shrug your shoulders and think, "That wasn't really such a big deal!"

• Make one or several positive affirmations to affirm your new decision. In the days after you make a new decision, the original decision might come back to haunt you. Each time that happens, be alert and do not allow your mind or emotions to start going over the situation again. Simply decide to stop your mind and emotions from going into the old track. Don't allow your mind to act as a broken record. Instead, repeat your positive affirmation, mentally or verbally, and keep doing so until you no longer feel that your mind is being drawn back to the original situation. Make an affirmation that affirms the positive opposite of the original decision. In other words, if your original decision was, "I can't draw," make an affirmation stating, "I am a good artist and I enjoy drawing!"

You might have to apply these steps many times in the first few days after you make a new decision. In some cases, it might take weeks before your memory of the original situation fades away. However, if you keep affirming the new decision, the old one will eventually fade from memory. Remember that you are breaking an old, worn-out habit and replacing it with a new and better one. This will take time and require repetition.

Constancy is the key to victory

Keep in mind that your subconscious mind can have many layers of very complex computer programs. Too many people make a halfhearted attempt to resolve their psychological hang-ups and then they give up before the results start manifesting. Don't let this happen to you!

The tools presented here will work, and they will produce results. However, because your subconscious mind is like an onion that has many layers, the results will not happen overnight. The only way to manifest results is to keep taking one small step at a time. A small step is very doable, and for that reason it might not produce dramatic results.

You might think of your personal path as the process of building a pyramid. A pyramid is built by stacking many small stones on top of each other. Each stone might seem like an insignificant step, yet if you keep adding stones, you can build a very impressive structure. On the other hand, if you tried to move all of the stones at once, you would break under the strain.

Building a new self-image
If you will remain constant, you will eventually consume all toxic energy generated after you made that original decision. You will also start building a constructive subconscious program to replace the toxic program. You can enhance this process by building a new self-image based on your new decision. Visualize yourself as already being the person that you want to be. Create affirmations that affirm your new self-image, and start acting as if you already were that person. By doing this, you can start building a new sense of identity. In part two, you will receive a much deeper understanding of how to become who you really are.

Conclusion
The tools you have received in part one can produce significant results, and for now they might be all you need. If you apply them, they can take you to a much higher level on your personal path. As you move higher, you will begin to feel the need for a deeper understanding of who you are and why you are here. Part two will offer some keys to achieving this understanding.

PART TWO:
A Spiritual Approach to Personal Growth

Introduction

The discourses in part one are designed to give you a set of practical tools that will empower you to anchor yourself firmly on the inner path. If you will embrace and apply the threefold approach of transforming toxic energies, replacing subconscious computer programs and learning to make better choices, you can make tremendous progress.

As you ascend on your personal path, you may begin to ponder the deeper questions of life. The discourses in part two are designed to help you gain a deeper understanding of who you are, so that you can find your own personal answers to life's questions. By using these discourses as a foundation and applying the inner approach to knowledge, you can gradually find meaningful, personal answers.

Why is it important to consider these questions when many people believe they have no answers? Because if you apply what you learned in part one, you will swiftly reach a point (if you have not reached that point already) from where you can make no further progress until you wrestle with these questions. As you go on, please don't forget about the basics. If you do not deal with toxic energies and subconscious computer programs, you might never find the answers to the deeper mysteries of life. If your consciousness is filled with toxic energies or unnecessary computer programs, you might not have sufficient room to receive the understanding that your higher self is waiting to bring into your outer consciousness.

The path is universal

In order to make the discourses in part one as universal as possible, spiritual topics are described in a manner that is not tied to a particular organization or belief system. This was done out of respect for those who do not consider themselves to be religious and to avoid offending anyone who has strong feelings for a particular religion. These goals have also been applied in part two. However, you cannot address the fundamental questions of life without touching upon spiritual topics. Once again, these discourses do not aim to create a new doctrine that will challenge or compete with existing doctrines. The book is not meant to tell you what to believe or not to believe.

The goal of these discourses is to illumine the inner path which transcends the outer divisions that humankind has created throughout the ages. You can follow this inner path no matter who you are, what outer group you belong to or what beliefs you might have. If you are not religious, the path does not require that you join any particular religion. If you belong to a particular religion, and feel strongly about that religion, the inner path does not require you to abandon it. If you have grown up in a particular culture, be it religious or otherwise, the path does not require you to remove yourself from that culture.

Sharing your insights

Following the path can be a completely private matter, because personal growth is a process that takes place inside yourself. No one else needs to know that you are following this path. As you begin to get insights from your higher self, you might gain an understanding that goes beyond your present beliefs. However, you do not need to tell anyone about your new understanding. In fact, you should remain silent or tell only people whom you feel are open to this deeper understanding. Therefore, you do not need to go out and challenge existing doctrines or seek to convince other people about anything.

However, when you do feel like sharing your progress and your understanding with other people, remember that free will is the basic law of this universe. Why seek to force an idea upon someone or tell others what they should believe. Instead, you might encourage them to develop their own understanding by applying the inner approach to knowledge.

As you read the following discourses, keep in mind that these teachings are given with the clear recognition that only ideas coming from your higher self will make a difference in your life. Therefore, these discourses will present ideas to stimulate the process whereby you get insights from your higher self. You are not required to believe any specific doctrine in order to benefit from these discourses. The only requirement is that you are willing to apply the inner approach to knowledge.

DISCOURSE 7:
The Fall of Man and Woman

Throughout recorded history, religion has been part of life on this planet. Obviously, religion could not have survived for so long unless it benefitted people in some way. One reason religion appeals to people is that many religious teachings deal with topics that are not specifically spiritual. Such teachings offer valuable insights into the process of everyday living.

Many religious teachings also contain valuable insights into human psychology, and these insights can be helpful to people no matter what they believe or do not believe. In other words, if you are truly interested in the inner path, the psychological lessons that can be gleaned from many of the world's religions are invaluable. In the coming discourses, we will apply a universal approach to religion and seek out ideas that can shed new light upon the questions of who you are and why you are here. As you will see, the insights we can glean from this universal approach are profoundly related to the topics that were discussed in part one.

When you look at the religions found on this planet, you see an incredible diversity. Many are blinded by this diversity, so they focus on the individual trees and are unable to see the forest. Let us take one, or rather several, steps backward and look at the overall picture of humankind's religions. Can we find certain trends or ideas that are shared by a large number of religions?

As we begin to look for such universal elements, one particular idea immediately springs to mind. Many of the world's religions contain the idea that humankind as a whole has become "lost" and that people have sunk, fallen or descended into a state that is lower than what they had at some earlier time. This concept clearly parallels some of the ideas that were discussed in part one, namely, that people have lost contact with their higher selves and have become trapped in the lower part of their minds.

Is it possible that humankind has become lost because people have lost their conscious contact with their higher selves? Is it possible that humankind as a whole has sunk into a lower state of consciousness in which people no longer remember their true, inner identity and their origin in a higher octave? Is it possible that the Fall of Man was a fall in the vibration of people's consciousness, so they no longer see their higher selves? Let us explore these questions by performing a thought experiment.

Creating worlds and souls

Imagine that you are a spiritual being with the power to create. You can create anything that you can envision or imagine. You decide to create an intricate and complex system of worlds, and you begin by creating a basic substance that can be shaped into any imaginable form. Therefore, you say, "Let there be light!"

You do not intend to create a static world but a world that is constantly evolving or growing. To make sure that your world will not self-destruct, you set up certain principles, or laws, that guide its evolution. After a few experiments, you define a set of principles that are so sophisticated that your world can evolve almost without any assistance from you.

Your world has several layers, or levels. You begin by creating the highest octave and it is made from light of a very pure and high vibration. After this, you create the next octave, which has a slightly lower level of vibration. You keep repeating this process until you have a number of octaves, each with a successively lower level of vibration. One might call your creation the "world of form."

You are not satisfied with being an outside observer looking at what you have created. You want your creation to evolve in ways that are surprising to you, and you want to know what it is like to live inside of your creation. To accomplish this goal, you create a number of spiritual beings. These beings are created in your own image and likeness. Therefore, they have the capacity of consciousness to know you as their spiritual parent, and they have the ability to create within the laws you have defined.

Because your spiritual children are created for the specific purpose of experiencing and participating in the world of form, they have a dual nature with the following elements:

- Your children have a spiritual self that enables them to know you and recognize that they are your offspring. This spiritual self is an individualization of you, and it enables your children to know your laws. You have written your laws in their inward parts.

- Your children each have a soul, and the souls enable them to experience the world of form from the inside by participating in that world. Whereas the spiritual self permanently resides in the highest octave of the world of form, the soul can descend into octaves of a lower vibration. The soul is not an outside observer but a participant in the drama you have created.

You decide to create a world that can evolve in unforeseen ways, and you want your children to surprise you with their creative abilities. Therefore, you give your children the ability to act as co-creators. Obviously, your children's creative abilities are not unlimited. They have the ability to create within a certain framework that prevents them from destroying themselves or the world in which they live. You want your children to start with limited creative abilities, and as they gain more experience, they can receive greater and greater abilities. When they have proven to be faithful over a few things, you intend to make them rulers over many.

The relationship between the spiritual self and the soul is that the spiritual self serves as the anchor point for the soul's journey into the lower levels of the world of form. The spiritual self is like a sun, and the soul is like a planet orbiting that sun. The spiritual self is the nucleus of the atom of self, and the soul is an electron orbiting the nucleus.

As the creator, you know that you cannot create anything without choosing what to create; therefore, you give your children the gift of free will. Because it is the soul that travels into the world of form, the soul is the seat of that free will. The soul chooses what to create, and the spiritual self gives the soul the understanding of how to create in harmony with your laws. As long as the soul has conscious contact with the spiritual self, the soul will know your laws. Therefore, the soul can make choices that are not self-destructive.

Traveling into the world of form

Some of your spiritual children express a desire to descend into the octave that is known as the material octave, or the material universe. The process whereby a soul descends into a lower octave is comparable to a planet shifting into an orbit that is further away from the sun or an electron jumping into an orbit that is further away from the nucleus. As the soul moves further away from the center of being, the gravitational pull becomes weaker. In other words, the bond that ties the soul to the spiritual self decreases in strength. This is not a problem until the soul descends into the material octave.

In any of the higher or spiritual octaves, all energy vibrates at such a high level that it is easy for a soul to see that the octave is part of a larger whole. In other words, souls will always know that the spiritual octaves are expressions of a higher reality, namely you (as the creator). As a result, a soul abiding in a spiritual octave can never lose her connection to the spiritual self.

When the soul travels into the material octave, she crosses a threshold, or dividing line. The material octave is made from energies of such a low vibration that it becomes difficult for the soul to see these energies as an expression of higher or spiritual energies. In fact, some of the energies in the material octave vibrate at a level that makes them seem as a solid substance (matter) instead of pure energy. Therefore, a soul abiding in the material octave might not realize that the material universe is part of a larger whole, and the soul might lose contact with her spiritual self. If this were to happen, the soul would no longer have any direct knowledge of the principles that guide the evolution of the material universe. Therefore, the soul would be likely to make choices that are self-destructive. Obviously, you do not want to see this happen to your children. What can you do to make sure that your children do not become lost in the material world?

The cosmic schoolroom

You decide to create a schoolroom, a kind of mystery school, which is designed to prepare your children for life in the material universe. The mystery school is like a beautiful garden which has everything your children need. The garden also has a teacher, namely a spiritual being acting as your representative.

The Fall of Man and Woman

Your school has graded lessons, and souls start out by learning some of the easier tasks associated with life in the material octave. Then, they gradually rise to more difficult levels of instruction. Just before students are ready to graduate, they receive the most difficult lessons.

Because the soul is made from spiritual energies, she cannot act or express herself in the material universe. To live in the material octave, a soul must take on a physical body. The physical body is made from the type of energies that are used to build the entire material universe. Therefore, the body can act in this universe.

You have created an intricate physical body with an amazing number of capabilities. However, because the physical body is made from energies that vibrate at a much lower level than the energies of the soul, the soul finds it difficult to learn how to operate the physical body. In fact, the physical body is so complex that is has a kind of computer that runs the more basic bodily functions. In other words, a soul does not have to consciously tell the body to breathe or circulate blood. These functions, and many others, can be run by the body computer without any conscious interaction from the soul. This frees up the soul's awareness to experience the material universe and to express her creative abilities.

Unfortunately, there is a catch. The computer that runs the physical body, one might call it the "carnal mind" is made from the energies of the material octave. Therefore, it cannot perceive or understand that there is something beyond the material universe. The carnal mind has no concept of a higher world or higher laws, but understands only what it can observe. Because the energies of the material octave vibrate at a much lower level than the energies of the spiritual octaves, the carnal mind does not see that material energies are the expression of a deeper, fundamental reality. Therefore, the carnal mind does not recognize higher or absolute truth. To the carnal mind, everything is relative to the material universe. The carnal mind does not know good in an absolute sense; it only knows good as a polar opposite to evil.

When the soul descends into a physical body, she perceives the material world through the senses of that body. The physical senses can detect only the energies of the material octave. Therefore, the soul cannot physically see the spiritual world. Furthermore, the soul will inevitably be affected by the carnal mind. This mind cannot fathom the concept of a spiritual side to life. As a result, the soul might receive no outer help for keeping her connection to the spiritual self. She must maintain this connection entirely by her own efforts, and it must be an inner connection. While a soul lives in a spiritual octave, she has no need to worry about this inner connection, because everything around her serves as reminders of the spiritual side of life. Consequently, the descent into the material octave is a major change for the soul. If a soul is not fully prepared, she could be overwhelmed by the physical senses and the carnal mind to such a degree that she loses her conscious contact with the spiritual self.

Your cosmic schoolroom is designed to gradually teach the soul how to deal with this challenge. Every step of the soul's education leads up to the moment when the soul leaves the schoolroom and descends into a physical body. Every step is designed to prepare the soul to handle this challenge without losing her conscious contact with the spiritual self. You have done everything possible to make sure that no soul will take on the dualism and the relativity of the carnal mind until she has been properly prepared.

In fact, you have expressly forbidden the inexperienced students from experimenting with the carnal mind. If one were to describe this through a metaphor, one might say that your schoolroom is a garden with a number of trees that

The Fall of Man and Woman

bring forth wonderful fruits of knowledge. Your inexperienced students are free to partake of any of these fruits except for the one that comes from a tree that represents the relativity of the carnal mind. On might call this the fruit of the knowledge of good and evil, or rather, of relative good and evil.

If an inexperienced student were to partake of this fruit, that soul would almost inevitably lose her contact with the spiritual self. If that were to happen, the soul would die in a spiritual sense of the word. Therefore, this fruit is reserved for students in the graduate class.

Before you let your students graduate, they must demonstrate that they can take command over the carnal mind. The carnal mind is meant to be the obedient servant of the soul. However, the carnal mind is programmed to ensure the survival of the physical body, and therefore it has a tendency towards selfishness (which to the carnal mind is simply a matter of survival). To experience life in the material octave, the soul must pay a price—she must constantly keep the carnal mind in reigns. The soul must be the operator of the body computer, and she must never allow the carnal mind to run her life. Only when a student has demonstrated this capability can you let him or her loose in the "real" world outside your protected schoolroom.

A dangerous choice

For a long time everything goes fine, and your students pass the final exam with flying colors. They venture into the material world without losing contact with their spiritual selves, and when they have had enough, they safely ascend back to their home of light in a higher octave.

One day, some younger students get wind of the forbidden fruit that they are not allowed to eat. These souls believe that the grass is always greener on the other side of the fence and that forbidden fruit is always the sweetest. One night, they sneak out of the dormitory and climb over the fence into the schoolmaster's yard. They eat of the forbidden fruit, and at first they think it tastes pretty good. However, because they were not ready for the challenge, they become entrapped by the relativity of the carnal mind. This relativity is so subtle and pervasive that they do not fully understand what has happened. However, as the new day dawns, the students suddenly realize that they have lost the contact to their spiritual selves. They also realize that they are "naked," meaning that they have no way to hide the fact that they have eaten the forbidden fruit. They know that when they meet the teacher, he will instantly know what they have done. The big question now becomes, How does the soul choose to respond to this situation? The soul has two options:

- She can go back to the teacher, admit her mistake and ask for help to get back on track.

- She can hide from the teacher.

If the soul chooses the first option, she will be forgiven and will receive the help and training necessary to get back on the path of growth. Unfortunately, if the soul chooses the second option, things are more complicated.

Free will is one of the fundamental laws of your world of form, and therefore the teacher cannot seek out a soul that has turned away from him. The teacher must stand back and respect that the soul has chosen to hide from him. However, when a soul refuses to work with the teacher, the soul has no purpose for remaining in the cosmic schoolroom. She is not cast out of the garden; the carnal mind lowers the vibration of the soul's consciousness until she can no longer perceive the schoolroom. The soul's attention, her conscious mind, now becomes attuned to the vibrations of the material octave, and she can no longer see beyond that level of vibration. Therefore, instead of being in a protected environment with the constant, loving guidance of an enlightened teacher, the soul has enrolled herself in the school of hard knocks. The soul must now learn by making unenlightened choices and by experiencing the consequences of those choices. The world has become her teacher.

When a soul is left to perceive the world through the senses and the carnal mind, she can easily forget her spiritual origin. The soul begins to identify with the physical body and the material world, and she begins to think of herself as a material being rather than a spiritual being. She has lost her true sense of identity as one of your spiritual children. She has lost her innocence, her inner sense of identity.

A house divided

For a moment, step out of the thought experiment and consider how these ideas might explain the divisions and power struggles that humankind has experienced throughout the ages. When people lose the lodestone of the spiritual self, they have nothing left but the relativity of the lower self. They might very well believe that the truth they have chosen to accept is the ultimate or absolute truth, but in reality this is a pervasive illusion. No absolute truth could ever come from the relativity of the material universe and the carnal mind. Even when humankind has been given a true teaching from a higher octave, people have a rare talent for turning it into a relative doctrine and using it as a weapon against those whom they perceive to be different.

How many times has this world seen two persons who were ready to kill each other because of some disagreement over a relative truth. How many times have two persons argued about what is true, each of them, in reality, saying, "The relative truth I have defined is more true than the relative truth you have defined; therefore, you should submit yourself to my will and allow me to rule over you?" Go into your heart and consider how much suffering has been caused by this never-ending human power struggle. Are you tired of playing this pointless game? Do you have an inner longing for something better?

How to help lost souls

Let us step back into the thought experiment and imagine that you are the creator of a group of souls who have become lost. How can you help the souls that have become entrapped in the material world? You have given them free will, so you cannot force them to come home. You must somehow seek to inspire them to come home of their own choosing.

Fortunately, you have a built-in safety mechanism. A soul is made from the higher energies of the spiritual octaves. Therefore, a soul can never feel completely at home in the material universe. The soul cannot fully identify herself with a physical body, but will always have a subtle inner sense that something is missing and that there must be more to life. The soul also has a deep inner longing to be one with something outside herself and that something is the spiritual self, because without it the soul will never feel whole or complete.

Some people manage to silence this inner longing for a while. Others indulge in the pleasures of this world in an attempt to divert their attention from an inner feeling that they cannot consciously understand or explain. However, very few manage to permanently silence the inner voice. Eventually, when the soul has experienced all there is to experience in this world, the inner voice becomes so strong that the soul can no longer ignore it. The soul must now seek to deal with this inner longing, but because of her inability to reach beyond this world, she often seeks to do so through outer, material means, which can never satisfy the soul's longing for her spiritual home.

Because you truly desire to see all of your children return home, you create a variety of tools to help souls find a deeper understanding of life. These tools are given in the form of religious, or spiritual, teachings. Your intention is that such teachings will serve as stepping stones to help souls look beyond the relativity of the carnal mind.

Unfortunately, the relativity of the carnal mind can cause people to turn religion into a tool for division and strife. Therefore, some people become so entrapped by the outer aspects of a particular religion that they fail to see the universal purpose behind all religions. That purpose is a path that allows the soul to escape the prison of the material world and reclaim her true, spiritual identity. What can you do to help souls that have misunderstood the true purpose behind religion? In reality, you can do nothing, because you have given your children free will. If they choose to allow the relativity of the carnal mind to dominate their lives, you must simply wait and hope that eventually they will tire of this game.

The path

Let us now step out of the thought experiment and consider what it might teach us about life on planet Earth. Millions of people are unable to see a universal purpose behind religion and spirituality. They often argue about a particular interpretation of doctrine instead of reading between the lines. They approach spirituality through the relativity of the carnal mind instead of applying the inner approach to knowledge. Many people have become so attached to the carnal mind and the material world that they are unwilling to reach for their higher selves.

Since you are still reading this book, you are obviously willing to apply the inner approach to knowledge. This willingness is a sign that your soul is ready to reach beyond the carnal mind. Your soul is longing to reunite with the spiritual self and she, or rather you, will never be satisfied with anything less. Fortunately, there is a well-established path that you can follow.

In every society and generation, some people have managed to reach beyond the carnal mind, and they serve as examples for others to follow. Although some of these saints, sages or seers have often been members of a particular religious group, they have never allowed their path to be confined by the rituals and doctrines of that organization. In their hearts, they have reached beyond the outer facade, and they have discovered that beyond the outer divisions created by humankind is a universal teaching. This universal teaching states that the road to your spiritual home requires you to go beyond the carnal mind and reestablish a conscious contact with the higher self. The soul must wrestle her sense of identity out of the claws of mortality and materialism, and she must reclaim her true identity as a spiritual being, a being that is in this world but not of this world. This is the true inner path, and you too can follow it!

DISCOURSE 8:
The Anatomy of Your Inner Being

The thought experiment in the previous discourse was meant to illustrate that personal and spiritual growth is a process that takes place in your mind and soul; one might call it your inner being. Therefore, you can benefit greatly from developing a better understanding of your inner being. After all, you will find it easier to solve a problem when you know what you are up against. With our current understanding, it becomes much easier to outline the various elements of the inner being. Let us take a closer look at this intricate phenomenon.

If you are using the inner approach to knowledge, you already know that your being has several levels, or layers. The chart on the following page outlines the elements of your being that has been mentioned in these discourses.

The following sections will describe each element of your being in greater detail. As you read the description of each element, do not forget the big picture. The key elements of your being are the spiritual self and the soul.

You are a spiritual being, and you are meant to express your spiritual individuality in the material universe. You express this individuality through the soul, but you can only do so when your soul is in contact with the spiritual self. In other words, your individuality is anchored in the spiritual self and it is expressed through the soul. To express your individuality in this world, you need both elements and you need them to form a polarity. Your soul must be an extension of your spiritual self.

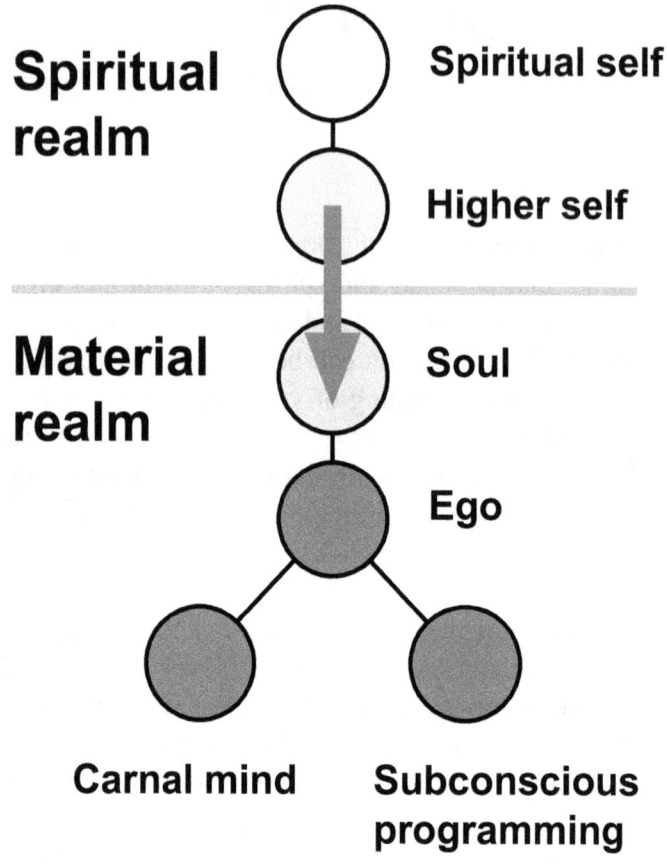

Because the seat of your free will is in the soul, specifically in the conscious mind, the soul must identify herself as an extension of the spiritual self. For only by so doing will the soul be kept in balance and avoid making self-destructive choices. The key to personal growth, the key to happiness and peace of mind, is to strive for a balanced and harmonious polarity between your soul and your spiritual self. The real purpose of the spiritual path is to reestablish your soul's conscious connection with the spiritual self.

As you gain a deeper understanding of your inner being, you begin to see that the spiritual self and the soul are the stars in the drama of your life. The other elements of your being are also players in the drama, but they have less important roles. These roles can be divided into two categories. Your higher self plays a supporting role and is the key to bringing about balance between your soul and your spiritual self. The lower parts of your mind all play nonsupportive roles and they will, by their very nature, seek to prevent you from uniting with your spiritual self. If you keep these dynamics in mind, the following description will be more meaningful and practical.

The spiritual self

Your spiritual self is the core of your being. It is residing in a higher octave, and it is completely pure and unaffected by any of the energies of the material octave. No matter what mistakes you might have made in this world, your spiritual self is complete, innocent and pure. Nothing could ever corrupt your spiritual self. The importance of this is that no matter what mistakes you think you have made, no matter what sins you think you have committed, nothing has corrupted or degraded the very core of your being.

Your spiritual self is as pure and innocent as the day it was first created. By applying the inner approach to knowledge, you can come to accept that your spiritual self expresses the perfection of the spiritual world, and therefore it is fully acceptable in the eyes of God. Your soul might have made wrong choices. However, by reuniting with the spiritual self, your soul can engage in the process of overcoming all past mistakes and paying back her debts to life.

A soul that is disconnected from the spiritual self can indeed be lost. But by reaching for the spiritual self and showing a true willingness to reunite with that self, the soul can redeem herself. A soul will not be lost as long as she maintains her contact with the spiritual self.

Your spiritual self has a unique individuality. The spiritual self makes you who you are, and it makes you different from any other human, or rather spiritual, being. Because your spiritual self is made from the energies of a higher octave, it can be compared to a spiritual fire or spiritual flame. Your personal flame is absolutely unique. You carry qualities in that flame that no one else can express but you. One of the purposes of your existence, and of your descent into the material octave, is to express your unique spiritual flame everywhere you go. By doing so, you will make an invaluable contribution to the progression of life in the world of form. At the same time, you will feel an inner fulfillment and a sense of purpose that you have never dreamt possible.

Your spiritual self is the source of all of your energies. It is the stream of spiritual energy from the spiritual self that keeps you, meaning the soul and even the physical body, alive. If a soul has cut herself off from conscious contact with the spiritual self, the stream of energy from that self has been reduced to a mere trickle. It is only enough to keep the soul and the physical body alive. However, as soon as the soul begins to reestablish conscious contact with the spiritual self, the stream of energy will be expanded. As you grow and as your contact with your spiritual self expands, you can receive an almost unlimited amount of energy from your spiritual self. This is the true meaning of personal empowerment, or rather spiritual empowerment.

As already mentioned, your spiritual self is the anchor point for your soul. Your soul should be like a planet orbiting around the sun of your spiritual self. If your soul accepts this role, she will automatically find a perfect orbit that will help you fulfill your spiritual goals. Through your spiritual self you have access to a full understanding of the spiritual and natural laws that are guiding the evolution of the world of form. Through that contact your soul gains right understanding, and therefore you can avoid making self-destructive or limiting choices.

This does not mean that the soul surrenders her free will to the spiritual self. Your soul is the seat of your free will and it is at this level that you make choices. It is important to understand that your spiritual self will not make those choices for you. What the spiritual self will do is give you a clear understanding of the situation in which you are making choices. In contrast, your carnal mind and your subconscious programming can override your free will and run your life for you.

In many cases, this inner guidance does not take the form of full outer knowledge of the various options and consequences. Instead, it often happens through an inner, intuitive experience whereby you know that one particular option is the right thing to do. However, the choice is still yours.

In most situations, you have several right choices. In other words, none of these choices will generate negative energy or self-destructive consequences. Therefore, you could just as easily choose one option as another, and in the end the choice truly is up to your conscious mind.

In contemplating your spiritual self, it is important to consider the concept of the will of God. Some theologians claim that humankind does not have free will because everything is subject to the will of God. In reality, it is the will of God to create spiritual beings that are not mechanical robots but beings with the ability to make conscious choices. Therefore, the exercise of your free will is mandated and allowed by the will of God. Obviously, God does not want you to make choices that are self-destructive or that destroy other parts of creation. Most certainly, God does not want you to make choices that are harmful to the other spiritual beings in your world. However, within the framework of the spiritual and natural laws that guide the world of form, God has complete acceptance of your right to make freewill choices. Therefore, one choice isn't necessarily right for everyone. The choice that is right for you is a choice that best expresses your unique, spiritual individuality and therefore anchors your spiritual flame in the material octave. In the coming discourses, we will take a closer look at these ideas.

The spiritual self is what gives you the ability to feel that you exist and that you are a conscious being with a distinct individuality. Because the spiritual self gives you the ability to recognize that "I am," some spiritual teachings have called the spiritual self the "I AM Presence." Contemplate this name in connection with the biblical statement that the name of God is "I AM THAT I AM."

Another function of the spiritual self is that it acts as a storehouse for the memories of the soul's victories and right choices. The soul can access these treasures laid up in Heaven and receive intuitive insights through which she knows what is enlightened self-interest.

The soul

If the spiritual self is the center point of your being, then the soul is the pivot point of your being. Everything in your life revolves around the freewill choices made by the soul. Everything in your life depends on, is affected by and is a product of the choices made by the soul.

As the seat of your free will, the soul has her own sense of identity. That sense of identity is subject to choices made by the soul. In reality, you are a spiritual being and the totality of your being is the spiritual self and your soul. However, if your soul chooses to disconnect herself from the I AM

Presence, she must build a new sense of identity. By building this new sense of identity, this pseudo identity, the soul might forget her true identity as a spiritual being. Therefore, as far as your soul is concerned, the new identity has become your only identity. In reality, you are what you are, namely a spiritual being. However, to the soul, you are what you think you are. You are what you see yourself as being. You are what your sense of identity says that you are.

Because the soul has free will and the potential to disconnect herself from the I AM Presence, you can describe the soul by talking about different stages, or states, of the soul:

- A soul that has no contact with the spiritual self (a lost soul).

- A soul that has partial contact with the spiritual self and is in the process of increasing that contact (a growing soul, a soul that is anchored on the inner path).

- A soul that has full contact with the spiritual self (an enlightened soul).

When a soul has conscious contact with the spiritual self, she identifies herself as an extension of the I AM Presence. The soul realizes that she is a spiritual being who is only temporarily abiding in the material octave. She realizes that she is in the world but not of the world. Through contact with the spiritual self, the soul has access to a full understanding of the spiritual and natural laws guiding the world of form. Therefore, the soul will always know whether her choices are in harmony with those laws. The soul can draw upon the memories of her previous experiences in the world of form.

Therefore, she can use those experiences as a foundation for making better choices.

When a soul has conscious contact with the spiritual self, the soul only needs the carnal mind to perform routine tasks that involve the functions of the body. The soul does not need the carnal mind to make right choices, because she can get the understanding she needs directly from the spiritual self. Therefore, an enlightened soul has put the carnal mind in its rightful place as a servant and she never allows the carnal mind to influence her choices.

The individuality of the soul is an extension of the individuality of the spiritual self. A soul in her original state can be compared to a child. She has unlimited curiosity, enthusiasm and joy. The soul has a sense of complete security because she knows that she has a loving parent within easy reach. The soul knows that the entire material universe is made of lower, and therefore less powerful, vibrations than the vibrations of the spiritual self. Because of its higher vibrations, the spiritual self can protect the soul from the dangers of this world. So the soul can have complete confidence in the spiritual self and its protection and feel free to explore the world of form without any fears or doubts.

This is one of the reasons Jesus stated that unless you become as a little child, you cannot enter the kingdom of Heaven. Jesus also said that the Kingdom of God is within you, meaning that it is not a physical place but a state of consciousness in which the soul knows her true identity. The goal of the spiritual path is for the soul to get back to her original innocence, so that she can fully accept the protection and guidance of the spiritual self.

Now let us consider what happens when a soul disconnects herself from the I AM Presence. The soul suddenly realizes that she is alone in a strange and frightening world. The soul is forced to make choices, yet she no longer has an understanding of the spiritual and natural laws guiding the world of form. That understanding always came from the spiritual self. The soul has no spiritual protection and finds that she is vulnerable, she is naked, and that she can be attacked by numerous forces roaming this world seeking whom they may devour.

Because of its separation from the spiritual self, the soul is no longer like an innocent, playful, and curious child. Rather the soul is plunged into a frightening situation, and she is faced with doubts and fears that she never had to deal with in the past. Therefore, the soul is not prepared for such a situation. However, to survive in this world, the soul must quickly develop a way to deal with the perils of life on planet Earth.

To cope with this new situation, the soul uses her creative abilities in an attempt to build what she had before. She therefore seeks to fashion a new form of mind that can replace the spiritual self. The soul hopes this new mind can provide the same services that the spiritual self used to provide. Unfortunately, the soul has to build this new mind out of the energies that are accessible to her, meaning the energies of the material octave. Therefore, this new mind can never provide the protection and guidance that the soul received from the spiritual self. However, as long as a soul refuses to go back and face her spiritual teacher and work on reestablishing her connection to the spiritual self, that soul has no other options. Therefore, she must continue to build what becomes a pseudo identity. This pseudo identity is formed as a result of the following process:

- The soul begins building a new sense of identity, and this sense of identity is based on the illusion that she is separated from the spiritual self. This new sense of identity is what becomes the ego.

- The soul seeks to develop a new foundation for making right choices. As a result of this, she develops a set of subconscious computer programs for dealing with the situations she encounter in life. Let us refer to these computer programs as the lower self.

Whereas the spiritual self stores the soul's positive memories, the subconscious mind becomes a storehouse for the soul's negative memories. These memories are all perceived through the senses of the physical body and the relativity of the carnal mind. Therefore, these memories are not a good foundation for making right choices.

The basic relationship between the soul and the I AM Presence dictates that your spiritual self must respect the freewill choices made by the soul. Therefore, it can do nothing to pull you out of the illusion that you are a material being or that you are isolated from the spiritual self. It can only continue to send you spiritual energy so that you can maintain life in your physical body.

In reality, the soul's separation from the spiritual self is an illusion that exists only in the mind. It is a product of the soul's self-destructive choices, and it can be undone by replacing those past choices with new and better choices. It can be undone by reclaiming the soul's true identity as a spiritual being.

Because you have free will, the only way to break this impasse, or stalemate, is for your soul to choose to reach beyond her pseudo identity. It is the soul that must reach up for the spiritual self because the spiritual self cannot reach down and force the soul to take the first step on the path. Once you make a decision to come up higher, your spiritual self can give you all kinds of assistance. But you, and you alone, must take that first step.

The homeward path can only begin when you make a conscious choice to reach beyond the lower self and the material world. The process can only be completed if you choose to continue to walk the inner path until you have reclaimed your spiritual identity and have come to fully accept that you are a spiritual being.

The ego and the subconscious computer

We earlier compared the subconscious mind to a computer. You are probably aware that a computer has a piece of software which is called the operating system. This piece of software is what gives the computer its identity as a UNIX, Macintosh, DOS or Windows computer. The operating system defines the general environment in which other pieces of software can operate. Likewise, the ego is the operating system of the subconscious computer.

The ego was originally created by the soul, and this took place when the soul lost contact with the spiritual self and found herself outside the mystery school. The soul created the ego in an act of desperation. Throughout the existence of the soul, she had never been alone. She had always been an extension of the spiritual self, and therefore the soul is only complete when she feels connected to something outside herself. When the soul lost her connection to the spiritual self, she was plunged into a sense of aloneness, a sense of being incomplete and a feeling of being abandoned. Because the soul could not bear this loneliness, she created a substitute, a surrogate, for the spiritual self.

The soul created the ego in an attempt to mimic the qualities of the spiritual self. The spiritual self and the soul are created in a perfect polarity. The spiritual self is yang, or masculine, in relation to the soul, which is yin, or feminine. Although the soul has free will and clearly makes her own choices, she makes those choices within the framework that is defined by the spiritual self. In other words, when the soul is in polarity with the spiritual self, she has a safe environment in which to make choices.

When the soul created the ego, she attempted to create a yang, or active, polarity to her own yin, or feminine, qualities. In other words, the soul wanted the ego to define the framework in which she could make choices. The soul wanted the ego to be somewhat in command of her existence.

Unfortunately, a soul that has lost contact with the spiritual self does not understand the concept of absolute right and wrong. Because the ego is created out of the energies of the material octave, the ego is likewise unable to distinguish between right and wrong in an absolute sense. To the ego, everything is relative and the framework that it defines for the soul is a relative framework. The ego does not understand or accept the concept of absolute truth or the laws of God. The ego thinks it can define its own rules and that it is a law unto itself.

The ego is, in a very real sense, a house built on sand, namely, the shifting sands of the energies of the material octave. Because of this, the soul began to make self-destructive and limiting choices. When the soul had to face the consequences and experience the pain and discomfort of those consequences, she gradually became afraid of making choices.

Therefore, the soul started creating a number of subconscious programs to help her deal with the situations she encountered in life, many of which were the results of her own wrong choices. These programs were created within the framework defined by the operating system of the ego. Therefore, they too were houses built on sand, and instead of solving problems as the soul had hoped, the subconscious computer programs only created more problems and

The Anatomy of Your Inner Being

more unpleasant consequences. Because the soul did not acknowledge the need to base her choices on the guidance of the spiritual self, she had no way to avoid making bad choices. Therefore, the soul kept building layers upon layers of subconscious computer programs designed to avoid or deal with the pain caused by her bad choices. Over time, a soul can build an almost infinitely complex conglomerate of subconscious computer programs. Because these computer programs are created to deal with situations that the soul encounters in the lower vibrations of the material octave, we might call these programs the "lower self."

The soul quickly found herself in a situation where it seemed as if every choice led to unpleasant or disastrous consequences. So the soul thought that she had no way out of her dilemma. In reality, the soul always has a way out, because the soul can turn around and reach for the spiritual self. However, as long as the soul upholds her original decision to turn away from the spiritual self and her spiritual teacher, the soul does not have a way out of her own self-created misery.

Because of her wrong choices, the soul experienced an increasing intensity of emotional pain, fear, doubt, anger, frustration, self-hatred, lack of self-confidence and a host of other negative emotions. To cope with the increasing pain, the soul became an introvert. She started to withdraw from the world, and thereby she allowed the ego and the subconscious computer programs to run her life. Obviously, this only made the situation worse, but the soul eventually managed to bury herself so deeply under layers of denial that she became almost numb to the pain.

What could break the stalemate of the soul? What could take the soul down from the cross on which she had been crucified by the ego and the lower self? The soul cannot pull herself up by her own bootstraps; she cannot free herself from the situation she has created, and obviously the ego and the subconscious computer programs cannot set her free either. The only possible solution is that the soul has to receive help from outside herself, outside the ego and outside the lower self. This help can only come from higher octaves. As we shall see shortly, this help is available to all.

As you begin the process of reclaiming your spiritual identity, you need to be aware of one particular aspect of the ego. We have compared the ego to the operating system of a computer, but it is a very sophisticated operating system. In fact, it is so sophisticated that is has a certain state of consciousness. This consciousness allows the ego to know that it exists and that it owes its very existence to the soul.

In reality, the ego can only continue to exist as long as you feed it by misqualifying the energy coming from your spiritual self. Because the ego is created from lower energies, it has no ability to receive energy from a higher octave. The ego cannot live from the pure, spiritual energies that come from your spiritual self. The ego can only absorb energies of a lower vibration, which means that someone most lower the vibration of the spiritual energy. That someone is your soul, and you lower the vibration of spiritual energy by engaging in negative thoughts or emotions.

As long as you engage in negative or limiting thoughts, feelings and actions, you continue to feed the ego. Therefore, the ego does not want you to break free of such negative habits. It wants to keep you trapped in a state of consciousness that causes you to feed it energy. Furthermore, the ego cannot fathom or accept the idea of a spiritual self, and it considers this idea to be unreal or erroneous. The ego does not see anything beyond the material world. The ego will actively seek to keep you trapped in the illusion that you are a material being, and the ego will use all of its influence to keep you, meaning the soul, in chains. Therefore, you must realize that in the ego you encounter a very real inner opposition to your progress on the spiritual path.

This does not mean that you should fear that you have some kind of Frankenstein's monster in your subconscious mind. Once again, being forewarned is being forearmed, and by realizing that the ego will resist your progress on the path, you can avoid being ensnared by its manipulations. The key to escaping this manipulation is, as always, to follow the voice of your higher self. However, before we take a closer look at that higher self, let us consider the final aspect of the lower self.

The carnal mind

As we saw earlier, the carnal mind is like a computer that is designed to run the physical body. Its primary responsibility, or modus operandi, is the long-term and short-term survival of the body. In practical terms, this means food, propagation and protection. The carnal mind has no moral or ethical standard whatsoever. It is completely centered around performing the tasks it was designed to do, and it will do so with absolutely no regard for how its actions affect other forms of life. The carnal mind will do anything to defend the life of the body, including killing any number of other human beings who seem to threaten the body. The carnal mind will do anything to provide food for the physical body, including killing and stealing to obtain that food. The carnal mind will do anything to satisfy its sexual desires, including violence and rape.

Despite these self-centered, immoral and unethical tendencies, the carnal mind is not necessarily the enemy of the soul. The carnal mind is like a computer, and as such it has no understanding of the consequences of its actions. If a computer is programmed to target a nuclear missile at a city with ten million people, it will fire that missile with no understanding of the consequences of that action. Likewise, the carnal mind will do whatever it takes to ensure the survival of the body, and it has no understanding of the consequences of its actions.

Therefore, the carnal mind was originally meant to be kept under strict control by the soul. Because the soul had direct contact with the spiritual self, the soul had an absolute standard for deciding what was right. If the soul withdraws from reality and refuses to take command of her situation, then she obviously cannot keep the carnal mind under control. On the other hand, the carnal mind cannot function on its own, just as a computer cannot do anything without an operator. When the soul withdraws, the carnal mind is a computer in search of an operator. Therefore, the ego and the lower self now take on the role of operating the computer of the carnal mind. Once again, the ego and the lower self have no absolute standard for deciding moral and ethical questions. Therefore, they form an unholy alliance with the carnal mind, and to a large degree they allow the carnal mind to do its thing.

This explains why some people can become so self-centered that they do whatever they want regardless of the consequences for other people. Although the human body is a more sophisticated device than the body of any animal, the computer that runs the human body is essentially no different from the computer that runs the body of a higher animal. Therefore, if a human being, a human body, is controlled by the carnal mind, that person is, in a very real sense, functioning at the animal level.

Once again, the only escape for the soul is to start putting her house in order and take command over the carnal mind, the lower self and the ego. Obviously, the soul is not strong enough to do this on her own; therefore, she needs help from above. Fortunately, the creator of the universe is not blind to the plight of the soul. From the very beginning, an escape route was built into the system.

The higher self

You might have noticed that these discourses have talked about a spiritual self and a higher self. The higher self is not the same as the spiritual self. In fact, the higher self is meant to be a mediator between the soul and the spiritual self.

The spiritual self, or the I AM Presence, cannot reach down into the low vibrations of the material octave. His eyes cannot behold iniquity. As long as the soul maintains a conscious contact with the spiritual self, that self can interact with the soul. However, this contact can only be maintained as long as the soul reaches beyond the material world. If the soul becomes entrapped by the ego, the lower self and the carnal mind, she can no longer reach beyond the vibrations of this world. Therefore, the spiritual self has no way to break through the energy veil, the illusion or maya that entraps the soul.

The higher self has the ability to bridge the gap in vibration between the material octave and the spiritual self. The higher self can provide a connection between the two aspects of your being, and it can act as a messenger from your spiritual self. The higher self is, so to speak, sent into the material world to save the soul and bring her back home. It is meant to be the personal savior of the soul. Some spiritual teachings call the higher self the "Christ Self."

Obviously, the soul still has to make a freewill choice to accept the direction and help of the higher self. When the soul can no longer hear the voice of the spiritual self, the soul can still hear the voice of the higher self. This voice is the still small voice within that calls the soul to come up higher.

It is often called intuition, but it is a form of intuition that one might call higher reasoning. The higher self does not tell the soul what to do; it reasons with the soul in an attempt to make the soul understand what is in her own best interest. The higher self says, "Come, let us reason together."

The soul can choose to ignore the inner voice, but she can never shut it off. To the soul, the higher self is literally the "door which no man can shut." Therefore, no matter how far the soul might have fallen into the low vibrations of the material octave, the soul can never lose contact with the higher self. No matter what mistakes you might have made, no matter how much negative energy you have accumulated in your energy field and no matter how many false ideas or concepts you have come to believe, you will always have a way out. To find the way, you must listen to the voice of your higher self, which speaks to you in the silence of your heart. You must listen to the inner voice, the voice of intuition. If you are willing to listen, your higher self will gradually lead you higher until you begin to regain your direct, conscious contact with your spiritual self.

Most of the world's religions contain, in one form or another, the concept of a savior who has come to Earth to save your soul. If you are a Hindu, you might see this savior in the form of Lord Krishna. If you are a Buddhist, you will see the savior in the form of the Buddha. If you are a Christian, you will see the savior in the form of Jesus.

Unfortunately, Christianity has to a large degree forgotten the aspect of an inner savior and has identified the savior in the form of the person of Jesus. If you have grown up in a Christian culture, you would do well to take the inner approach to knowledge and contemplate this statement made by Jesus himself, "The works that I do, you shall do also." How could you possibly do the works of a spiritual master like Jesus Christ? What if part of Jesus' mission was to show you an example of what any human being can accomplish by following the inner voice, the inner Christ? What if Jesus was able to do his works because he had united with a universal state of consciousness? As previously mentioned, that state of consciousness can be called the higher self. It is also known as the universal Christ mind, or Christ Self.

The New Testament contains the admonishment to "Let that mind be in you which was also in Christ Jesus!" If you will contemplate this statement in light of the ideas presented in this book, you will gain an entirely new perspective on the mission of Jesus. This perspective will in no way diminish the importance of Jesus and his role as savior. On the contrary, it will make this role come alive to you in a new and more personal manner.

Understanding desire

The key to spiritual progress is to make right choices, and the key to making right choices is to take control over the jungle of desire. It will be infinitely easier for you to make right choices if your conscious mind is not constantly being bombarded by conflicting desires. Traditionally, some spiritual teachings have stated that all desires are wrong and that they work against your spiritual progress. Therefore, some spiritual seekers believe they must extinguish all desires, and this often becomes a very great strain for their souls.

The Buddha did not say that the cause of all suffering is desire. He said that the cause of all suffering is wrong desire, meaning a desire that causes the soul to become attached to the material world. If you were to extinguish all desires, what would compel your soul to move forward on the spiritual path? Instead, you can seek to replace all limiting or worldly desires with liberating or spiritual desires.

To free yourself from limiting desires, you must recognize the different types of desires:

Desires of God

Your spiritual parents have desires for all of their children. God never desired for you to fall into a lower state of consciousness and thereby forget your spiritual origin. Therefore, God desires you to be free of all limitations so that you can accept and express your spiritual identity. God desires you to be a co-creator and to help in the refinement and expansion of God's creation. God also desires for your soul to fulfill the desires that made her travel into the material universe. God desires your soul to return home out of her own free choosing.

Desires of your higher self

Your higher self has the same desires as God, but your higher self is very much focused on your soul's liberation from the lower state of consciousness. Therefore, it desires to see you overcome all illusions and all limiting beliefs. It desires to see you climb the spiritual path and never again take a backward step.

Desires of your soul

While some spiritual teachings claim that all material desires are wrong, the soul has legitimate desires that relate to the material world. The soul chose to descend into the material world because she wanted to experience what it is like to live at this level of God's creation. The soul also desired to express her spiritual flame in the material world. Some souls descended because of a desire to help their spiritual siblings find their way home. These desires are all legitimate, and if pursued correctly (without attachment) they will not enslave the soul. In fact, a correct desire that is fulfilled through correct means will free the soul to ascend to a higher level in the spirit-matter continuum.

Desires of your ego

The ego is sophisticated enough to have a certain rudimentary form of consciousness and therefore it also has desires. The ego's deepest desire is for recognition. Every other desire of the ego revolves around the need for recognition. In reality, your ego wants to be recognized as a worthy replacement for your spiritual self, and this is an impossible task. Therefore, your ego's desire for recognition can never be satisfied.

Because the ego cannot gain recognition from a higher source, it seeks to gain recognition in the material world. The ego reasons that if every human being on Earth recognizes the ego and affirms its worth, then God simply has to accept it. This is a flawed reasoning, but your ego will never acknowledge that fact. Therefore, the ego will seek to gain worldly recognition for as long as it can fool, frighten or flatter your soul into going along with it. But no amount of worldly recognition can ever satisfy the ego. You can spend an entire lifetime pursuing the ego's desires, but nothing you do will ever be sufficient. The ego's desires are like a bottomless pit that can never be filled.

Desires of your carnal mind

The carnal mind has a primitive form of desire (an unconscious desire), which centers around the physical body. The carnal mind will seek to make your soul pursue its desires, and if your soul does not take command of the situation, you can spend a lifetime pursuing carnal desires. As with the ego, the desires of the carnal mind can never be satisfied. The carnal mind will never get enough sex, food, money, power or whatever it thinks will ensure the survival and pleasure of the physical body.

Taking command over desires

To avoid being sucked into a bottomless pit of desire, you need to recognize that it is up to you to take conscious control over the desires that are pulling on you from all sides. Recognize that the carnal desires relating to the body and the ego's desire for recognition can never be satisfied. Therefore, you must choose whether you want to spend the rest of your life on an impossible quest or whether you want to concentrate on the true spiritual quest.

The key to taking command over desires is to recognize that your soul takes on desires from sources outside herself. If your soul takes on a carnal desire and accepts it as her own, the soul will think that she truly needs more sex, food et cetera. Trying to free your soul from all desires is virtually impossible and not very productive. Instead, you can learn to replace a lower desire with a higher desire.

You can start this process by recognizing that your soul has legitimate desires that relate to this world. For example, many religious people think that the desire for sex is wrong. However, the human body was created and designed by God's emissaries. Some souls desire to experience the activities that you can do with a human body, and one of them is sex. This is a legitimate desire, but the soul's desire for sex is very different from the carnal mind's desire for sex, which is self-centered and insatiable. Whereas the carnal mind and the ego have insatiable desires, all of your soul desires are satiable. The lower desires will always seek to bind you to an endless repetition of certain acts, such as sex or eating.

The Anatomy of Your Inner Being

Your soul desires will continue to change, and they will go through a transformation from lower to higher desires.

For example, at a certain level of your path, your soul might desire to experience the physical pleasure of sex. However, this desire will gradually become refined into a longing for the true, spiritual union between a male and female polarity, a union which can (if understood and practiced correctly) serve as a reminder of the soul's desire for spiritual union. Your soul is the feminine polarity of your spiritual self, and she is constantly longing to reexperience union with that self.

How can you best deal with a lower desire, such as a consuming desire for sex? You might start by seeking an inner understanding of how your carnal mind's insatiable desire for sex is limiting you and binding your soul to a treadmill of selfishness. You can then begin to choose whether you want to take back your life or continue to let it be dominated by insatiable desires. In this context, you must realize that an unfulfilled desire can generate misqualified energy that can accumulate in your energy field. Over time, this energy can form a vortex that exerts a very strong pull on your emotions and thereby on your soul. You are then pulled into a negative spiral of insatiable desire and you are compelled to seek more sex. Yet no matter how much sex you have, it never satisfies the desire, so you end up wanting more. The key to breaking this spiral is to transform the toxic energy, as described in part one.

You can also engage in the path of seeking greater contact with your spiritual self. Because your soul has lost contact with the spiritual self, she feels incomplete, and she might seek to deal with this incompleteness through a material desire. For example, engaging in sex might make you feel less incomplete or help you to forget the sense of being incomplete. As you gain greater contact with your spiritual self, your sense of incompleteness will decrease and so will your desire to engage in an activity that only serves as a surrogate for the real thing.

This process will empower you to take command over the carnal mind so that your desire for sex is no longer running your life. As you overcome the carnal desire for sex, you will gain a greater awareness of your soul's desire to experience spiritual union through sex. This will open up new, and far more rewarding, avenues of sexual enjoyment.

As you keep refining and raising the nature of your desire for sex, you will eventually come to understand that all of your legitimate soul desires can be satisfied in an ultimate sense. In other words, you may eventually fulfill your soul's desire for sex and no longer desire it. Instead, you will replace that desire with a desire that reaches beyond the material world. This process is not a loss for the soul, and it does not require the soul to give up anything. The soul realizes that she no longer has a desire for sex because she has now discovered a spiritual desire which is far more attractive.

Throughout history, some people have chosen to willfully abstain from sex by using a certain amount of force or discipline. For some people this can be a constructive approach, if done with spiritual insight. You only receive a certain amount of energy from your spiritual self, and you must choose how to use it. If you use it on sex, you cannot use it on spiritual activities. Therefore, for some people it can be beneficial to abstain from sex and concentrate on a spiritual activity. However, to complete your spiritual growth, you need to free your soul from the desire for sex (or any other material desire), and this cannot be done by denying the desire. It can only be done by replacing that desire with a spiritual desire.

This resolution must come from within. If you can reach this resolution by abstaining from sex (or any other material activity), then by all means do so. However, if you cannot, then do not force or condemn yourself. Instead, practice the activity in a responsible manner and seek to gradually refine the nature of your desire for that activity. This should naturally lead you to become less attached to the activity, and you might eventually get a clear inner feeling that it is time to give up the activity and move on.

Reclaiming your true, spiritual identity

How can you use this knowledge of the anatomy of your being to make progress on the spiritual path? The real goal of your spiritual path is to reclaim your spiritual identity so that your soul can go back to her original state of polarity with your spiritual self. To accomplish this goal, you must free yourself from the illusion that you are a material being, and you must free yourself from the false self-image that originated in the ego, the lower self and the carnal mind.

To overcome the pseudo identity, you, meaning the soul, must make conscious choices. You must gradually choose to let go of your false identity and rebuild your true identity. This is a process that can only be done in stages, and it will take time. However, if you truly understand how the ego, the lower self and the carnal mind have influenced your self-image, you can make this process much easier. After you begin to understand how these lower aspects of your being function, you can see through their attempts to control your life.

You might begin by seeing how the lower self affects your actions and causes you to do things that are selfish or self-destructive. You can then choose to remove the subconscious programs that cause you to commit such acts. As you begin to go deeper, you will begin to see how the lower self affects your thoughts and feelings. Once again, this recognition will help you choose to rise above the thoughts and emotions that spring from the lower self. Eventually, you will recognize how the lower self influences the very core of your soul, namely your sense of identity. You will begin to understand how your soul has built a false sense of identity as a being that is separated from God, as a sinner that can never be redeemed or as a person bound by limitations.

Based on this understanding, you can choose to go within and reach for a new self-image, a new sense of identity, that is based on the intuitive insights you get from your higher self. Eventually, you will regain your direct contact with your spiritual self, and thereby you will begin to tune in to your unique spiritual flame. As you recognize and understand that flame, you can begin to express it in this world. This empowers you to bring forth a unique spiritual gift that can make planet Earth a better place.

Raise the world by raising your consciousness

If this sounds a bit far-fetched, consider the previous teachings on how negative energy has to be stored somewhere. We have seen that negative energy is stored in your personal energy field. However, what if the Earth itself has an energy field and the toxic energies produced by humankind are stored in that field? When you consider the violence and atrocities that have been committed by human beings, you can imagine that a substantial amount of toxic energy is stored in the energy field of this planet. This energy is like a black cloud, and its gravitational pull makes it far more difficult for people to discover and follow the inner path. It has created a negative spiral for the entire human race.

The key to removing toxic energy is to direct a stream of high-frequency energy into the lower energy and transform it into spiritual energy. As you increase your contact with your spiritual self, the stream of spiritual energy coming from that self can be greatly increased. Thereby you become an electrode for spiritual light entering the material octave. This light will not only transform the toxic energy in your personal field, it will also help transform the toxic energy stored in the field of the entire planet. By removing this energy, you lighten the gravitational pull that affects the mind of every person on the planet. Your efforts will make it easier for other people to contact their higher selves and follow the spiritual path. As you become an open door through which spiritual light can stream into this world, you will begin to carry that light wherever you go. You will become a bearer of spiritual light, a lightbearer.

In addition to being an electrode of light, you can also bring a unique gift to the world. This gift will come through your spiritual flame which is unlike the spiritual flame of any other person. What is your particular flame? Only your higher self can show you this inner flame. If you engage in the process of contacting your higher self, you will gradually build a new sense of identity based on your spiritual flame. This will be the most adventurous journey you could possibly take, and it will give you a sense of meaning, purpose, mission, peace of mind and an intense inner joy that nothing in this world can take away from you.

DISCOURSE 9:
Understanding God

So far, these discourses have only skirted the topic of God and the existence of God. As you move higher on the spiritual path, you will need to resolve all conflicts in your concept of and relationship to God. Therefore, we will now bring the topic of God into the open.

Many sincere seekers find it difficult to relate to God in a personal way. This conflict is often caused by the fact that many people have an inner, intuitive sense of what God is like, yet they have grown up in a culture that describes God through an outer doctrine that you are not supposed to question. When you experience a conflict between the outer doctrine and your intuitive insight, it becomes difficult to balance the two. Hopefully, these discourses have demonstrated that such conflicts can be resolved by applying the inner approach to knowledge. You cannot resolve your relationship to God by studying outer doctrines, by using the relativity of the human intellect or the reasoning of the ego. However, if you are willing to look beyond outer doctrines and apply the inner approach to knowledge, your higher self will gradually help you resolve all conflicts in your relationship to God.

Why doesn't God prove his existence?

One of the major questions to resolve is whether God exists. Let us begin by reviewing a simple fact. For more than three centuries, materialistic scientists have attempted to develop theories to explain away the need for an intelligent creator. These theories have not yet explained how an incredibly

Understanding God

complex universe could have evolved through a process that is completely random and without intelligence. Therefore, an objective observer must conclude that science has not proven that God does not exist.

From a purely logical standpoint, one might raise the question, How could you ever prove that something does not exist? You can prove that something does exist, but you cannot prove that something does not exist. All you can say is that you have not found or proven the existence of God with the methods that have been employed up to this point. One can never rule out the possibility that new methods might be discovered that could prove the existence of God.

Many religious people find it difficult to understand why God has not settled the question once and for all. If you apply the inner approach to knowledge and contemplate the importance of free will, it becomes easy to answer this question. God has given human beings free will. In doing so, God has given them the ability to ignore or deny the existence of God. If God were to provide some unquestionable proof of his existence, then God would actually violate people's free will. By giving people free will, God has essentially given up the possibility of providing an unqestionable proof.

The conclusion one must reach is that, as of this moment, God does not desire to provide unquestionable proof. God has chosen to leave this up to the free will of the individual human being. In other words, the existence of God can only be proven on an individual level. In respect for the free will of the individual, God might never provide a worldwide, universal, unquestionable proof of existence. Such proof will be given on an individual basis to those who are willing to apply the inner approach to knowledge.

Throughout the ages, numerous people have proven, within themselves, that God does indeed exist. They have proven this not as a theory but as a direct inner experience that consumes all doubt. Some people have called this a mystical, or spiritual, experience. Whatever the name, the fact remains that any human being has the capacity to receive such an experience. Your soul can attain this experience through direct contact with your spiritual self. However, to receive this experience you must first open your mind and heart to God, and that requires you to resolve all conflicts in your view of God. One might say that this is what the inner path is all about.

Is God beyond the world of form?

We live in a world in which everything is defined by having some kind of form. If God created the entire world of form, it follows that God is beyond the world of form. The significance of this is that you cannot describe or picture God by using any ideas, words, concepts or images from the world of form. A description might illustrate some of the characteristics or qualities of God, but the only way to know God in an ultimate sense is to go beyond the world of form.

Consider the commandment "Thou shalt have no other Gods before me." Is this an attempt to prevent people from setting up an idol created in the world of form and thinking that the idol is outpicturing the totality of God? Is the commandment "Thou shalt not take unto thee any graven image" an attempt to help people find the true God by always seeking to look beyond any images from the world of form?

How can you know the God that is beyond the world of form? Only through a direct inner experience whereby you contact your spiritual self. Because your spiritual self, your I AM Presence, is an individualization of the presence of God, the I AM THAT I AM, it enables you to know the true presence of God. Throughout the ages, people from all cultures and traditions have had such spiritual experiences.

However, while these experiences are true, you cannot accurately describe such experiences by using words or images. You cannot describe what it is like to experience God. You can try to describe such an experience in an attempt to encourage other people to seek their own inner experiences; however, the description of a mystical experience should never be turned into an unquestionable doctrine. It should never be seen as an ultimate description of God. It should be seen as an incentive that can inspire people to seek their own personal experience.

Unfortunately, the relativity of the lower mind has caused people to create and accept many concepts about God that have nothing to do with the reality of the divine being. People have ascribed human characteristics, and thus human imperfections, to God and this has caused much conflict in the minds of many sincere seekers.

Contemplate the saying that God is not mocked, meaning that God is not affected by human beliefs or opinions. God is who God is, just as the Earth was round when people believed it was flat. You can know the reality of God, but to do so you must be willing to look beyond the imperfect and limited concepts created by human beings.

Did God create evil?

Many people ask the question, "Why is there evil in the world?" Traditionally, theologians have found it difficult to answer this question. If everything in the universe is in accordance with God's will, then it must be God's will that there is evil in the world. Yet this viewpoint does not ring true to a lot of people, because they have an intuitive sense of what God is like. If God has created everything, then it follows that God must have created evil, and some religions teach that evil is the polar opposite of God. Once again, this does not ring true to many people.

Because we have recognized the importance of free will, we can gain an entirely different perspective on the existence of evil. Evil was not created by God; it was created by conscious beings, including but not limited to, human beings. These beings used their free will to go against God's laws. God could not give people free will without giving them the ability to violate the laws used to create the world of form. The existence of evil is not in accordance with the divine blueprint, and God did not create evil. Yet God gave people free will and God allows people to misuse that free will to create evil. Nevertheless this does not mean that God wants people to create evil.

If people could not go against God's laws, they would not truly have free will. Yet if they do go against the laws used to build the world of form, they will eventually self-destruct. God's laws are designed to keep the world of form evolving in a sustainable manner, and anything that violates God's laws is not ultimately sustainable. Obviously, it is not in accordance with God's original intention that human beings use their free will to destroy themselves or to destroy parts of God's creation.

Even though free will is God's will, the results of the misuse of that free will are not in accordance with God's intention. Nevertheless, God allows human beings to create imperfect manifestations even while continuing to hope that they will someday realize that they are not acting in their own best interest. God is hoping that people will see the folly of their ways and decide to realign themselves with their true spiritual identity. Thereby, they can start exercising their free will in a way that is not self-destructive.

Anything that is created against the basic laws of God is predestined to self-destruct. Therefore, evil is only a temporary manifestation, a house built on sand. It will only last for a season before it destroys itself. God is not mocked, because all of the energy used by the forces of evil will eventually be raised to its original purity. To a human being, evil might seem to go on forever, but from a cosmic perspective it will be gone in the blink of an eye. People wonder how certain horrendous acts could possibly be erased. Yet to God the material universe might seem like a giant sandbox in which human beings play with God's energy. Whatever human beings have done can be erased by purifying the energy, just as the most elaborate castle built of sand can be erased by one wave rolling in from the ocean.

When God gave human beings free will, God must have known the potential consequences. Therefore, inexperienced souls start out in a world with a built-in safety mechanism. Because the material world is built from low-vibration energy, nothing in this world has permanence.

Human beings might take great pride in the castles they build on the beach, just as certain evil forces might think they have disturbed God's plan. Yet God knows that these forces have built their castles at water's edge during low tide. When the tide rolls in, even the most elaborate castles will be erased by one wave of spiritual energy rolling in from the cosmic ocean.

The concept of God's law

Some religions seem to teach that God is an angry and judgmental God who is constantly seeking to punish his offspring. Many people have a subconscious fear that they have been abandoned or punished by God. Some people think they are such great sinners that they could never be forgiven by God. Are these ideas true?

Imagine a person who is pounding his head against a concrete wall. Would you say it was the builder's fault that the person gets a concussion? The builder simply built the wall and he had no intention of forcing people to pound their heads against it. People have free will, and they have the right to pound their heads against a concrete wall if they want to. However, does it make sense for people to blame someone else for the fact that they have chosen to pound their heads against the wall?

God created a set of laws because without guiding principles the universe could not evolve in a sustainable manner. God also gave people free will, but God did not intend for people to use that free will to harm themselves (or others). Therefore, does it make sense to say that God punishes human beings? Or do people punish themselves by misusing their free will?

When a soul has turned away from her spiritual teacher, that soul can only learn by reaping the consequences of her actions. When a soul is not open to inner instruction, that soul has become her own teacher and the material universe is a schoolroom in which the soul can experiment. Hopefully, that soul will eventually begin to look for a deeper understanding of how the universe works. Hopefully, this quest for understanding will eventually lead the soul to rediscover her true identity.

The divine duality

Because God created man in his or her own image and likeness, you can understand certain characteristics of God by studying God's creation. This does not mean that God, in the ultimate sense, looks like an old man with a white beard sitting on a great throne (however, a representative of God may well look like this image). What can be learned from observing the world of form is that everything seems to spring from the creative tension between two elements that form a polarity. We see a polarity between matter and energy, between mind and matter, between the material world and the spiritual world, between male and female, and so forth. This fundamental polarity is beautifully illustrated in the Taoist symbol of the Tai Chi.

This symbol represents the two basic forces that create the world of form, namely an active (yang, or male) element that acts and a passive (yin, or female) element that is acted upon. The two elements are not opposites and they are not mutually exclusive. Instead, they complement each other and one could not exist without the other. It is the creative tension between these elements that gives rise to the entire world of form.

The human concepts of relative good and evil do not form a creative polarity. These mutually exclusive concepts cannot create anything, because they counteract and eliminate each other.

God has no opposite, but God does have a dual nature. One element of God's nature is the passive element. This can be seen as a state of pure being which has no form. Some spiritual teachings describe it as "the void" because to someone from the world of form it appears formless, or void. The other element of God's being is the active element, which can be seen as a spiritual being who is conscious of its own existence and of its ability to create. This being named itself with the words "I AM THAT I AM!"

The I AM THAT I AM uses its creative ability to act upon the state of pure being. Thus, everything is created from God's being, or essence. Without God was not anything made that was made. God created everything from one substance because God had nothing else to create from. God could not create something that was separate or different from God.

Everything in the world of form is the formless being of God who has temporarily taken on a disguise as something that has form. As you grow on the path, you begin to see that everything in this world is truly created from God's essence and energy. Because of free will, God has allowed human beings to create imperfect manifestations that are not in accordance with the divine blueprint. However, no matter how distorted the outer appearances may be, everything is made from God's energy. Therefore, even the greatest imperfections can be purified by raising the vibration of the energy to its original level.

The illusion of separation

Because everything is created from God's substance, it follows that nothing is truly separated from God. Imagine that you are flying in a helicopter, looking down at the ocean. At first, the ocean seems completely flat. No wind is stirring up the waves and therefore the surface of the ocean is like a mirror. Now imagine that a wind starts blowing. The wind creates waves, and as the wind blows harder, the waves become bigger. The waves might appear very different from the mirror-like ocean, yet they are created out of the basic substance of the ocean. No matter how big the waves become, they can never be separated from the ocean itself. Waves are not a fundamentally different creation; they are the ocean expressing itself in a different state. You cannot take a wave away from the ocean, because a wave does not exist without the ocean. Likewise, the world of form exists only because of the pure, formless essence from which it was made.

When your soul lost her conscious contact with the spiritual self, the soul felt like she was cut off from God. Because the soul experiences the world partly through the senses and the carnal mind, it is easy for the soul to believe that the entire material universe is separated from God. This has given rise to two widespread misconceptions. Many souls deny the existence of God, while others think that God is found somewhere "out there." Both of these beliefs are illusions.

Because everything is created from God's substance, nothing is actually separated from God. God is omnipresent, meaning that God is found in every part of creation, including the most seemingly God-forsaken places on planet Earth. There is no place where an omnipresent God cannot be found.

At a certain level on the spiritual path, it is natural to believe that the goal of the path is to overcome the soul's separation from God. The path then becomes a road to reunion with God. However, as you mature on the path, you will begin to realize that the true goal of the path is to overcome the illusion that the soul was ever separated from God. That separation is an illusion upheld by the carnal mind and the ego. In reality, your soul could never be separated from God any more than a wave could be separated from the rest of the ocean.

How God created the universe

The world of form resulted from the creative tension between two aspects of God's nature, namely the passive element of pure being and the active element of the I AM THAT I AM. As the first act of creation, God said, "Let there be light!" Light, or energy, became the basic substance from which the material universe was formed.

Light is a passive element, and it cannot create in and of itself any more than a lump of clay can form itself into a sculpture. Light can only form a material universe when it is acted upon by an active element. The active element is a being who is conscious of its own existence and of its creative ability. For light to become fashioned into a specific form, a conscious mind must imagine that form and hold a mental blueprint of the form. This blueprint becomes the mold, and when the creator sends forth the creative impulse, light flows into the mold and solidifies into the form envisioned by God.

To create the world of form, the I AM THAT I AM formed an image in its imagination and then projected this image into the passive element of light. Light, being passive, took on the form envisioned by the I AM THAT I AM. God is a sculptor working with the cosmic clay of light.

When God created the universe, God repeated the pattern of two polarities that create out of themselves. Therefore, God first created the highest level of the world of form, the highest of the spiritual octaves. In this octave, God created two polarities. These polarities were not mechanical forces. The I AM THAT I AM created them in its image and likeness as two spiritual beings who are fully conscious of their existence and of their role in creation.

The I AM THAT I AM does not create everything through its own efforts. From the very beginning, the I AM created conscious beings who acted as co-creators. The Bible states that the universe was created by Elohim, which is a plural word. The I AM is like the master architect who fashions the overall blueprint for creation. Yet many of the details of that creation are designed and determined by the spiritual beings who act as emissaries of the I AM.

Although the I AM has defined the basic framework for creation, it allows its co-creators to decide upon many of the details. In other words, the co-creators have free will and can choose how to implement the details of the larger framework. Because the co-creators are consciously aware that they are an extension of the I AM, they naturally do everything in full accordance with the basic framework defined by the I AM. Because their creation is in accordance with the original vision, it will not self-destruct.

We now see that the I AM has created a hierarchical structure. The I AM THAT I AM first created the highest spiritual octave and spiritual beings who reside at that level of creation. These spiritual beings, in the Bible called Alpha and Omega, created lower levels of creation and spiritual beings inhabiting those levels. From the highest level of creation to the lower levels of creation, the worlds become increasingly dense. In other words, the forms at the highest levels of creation are very fluid, or ethereal. Towards lower levels, the forms become more unchangeable, and they seem more solid, or dense. Furthermore, Alpha and Omega have almost unlimited powers to create, but towards lower levels, the co-creators have more limited creative powers. In other words, the beings at a given level create within the framework set by the levels above it.

Co-creators

The material universe is just one level in God's hierarchical structure, and human beings are created the same way that spiritual beings at higher levels are created. Your spiritual self is created from the basic substance of pure being. In other words, you too are an extension of the I AM and a part of God's hierarchical structure. Therefore, you are meant to be a co-creator with God. However, a human being has only limited powers to create (compared to the beings from a higher level of creation). For example, human beings do not have the creative power to alter the basic matrix for this planet.

Within a certain framework, human beings do have the power to create their own reality. They also have free will to choose what to create. As long as human beings maintain a conscious contact with their spiritual selves, their creation will be in accordance with the spiritual and natural laws that guide this universe. Therefore, their creation will be sustainable and it will not self-destruct.

As already mentioned, because human beings were given free will, they had the capacity to turn away from their original spiritual identity. When that happened, they did not lose their creative powers. So human beings have created a world that is no longer in accordance with the original divine blueprint. That is why you see forces of imperfection, decay and death in this world. They did not exist when the Earth was in accordance with the divine blueprint. These forces only came into existence because human beings used their creative power to go against the divine blueprint.

How do you co-create?

Let us consider how the material universe was created. As already discussed, everything in the world of form is created from God's substance, namely spiritual energy, or light. However, the material universe was not created from the highest form of spiritual energy. It was created from a more manifest form which vibrates within the frequency spectrum that is right above the material octave. A group of spiritual beings used this spiritual energy to create the material universe. How did they do this?

When the I AM THAT I AM started the process that led to the creation of the world of form, the I AM created an impulse that was expansive. One might say that the I AM breathed out, and this outgoing impulse is the driving force behind creation. You can envision this impulse as a stream of energy that flows from the I AM through all levels of creation. A group of spiritual beings residing in the octave right above the material octave became the directors of this stream of spiritual energy. Through their imagination and the power of their attention, they directed the spiritual energy and fashioned it into a certain form. For example, they envisioned planet Earth, and by keeping their attention focused on this vision for a period of time, they created the physical planet.

You are a co-creator, and you have a constant stream of spiritual energy flowing through your spiritual self into the lower part of your being, namely your soul. Even if you are not consciously aware of this energy, it is still flowing. Even if you do not realize that you are using this energy to create, you are nevertheless doing so. Therefore, whether you know it or not, whether you like it or not, you are constantly creating and you are doing so through your imagination and the power of your attention. Through your imagination, your mind envisions a certain form. The longer you keep your attention on that form, the more spiritual energy flows into it. Eventually, your vision will become a tangible manifestation. The material universe can be seen as a mirror, and it will reflect the ideas and concepts that you hold in your conscious or subconscious mind. Your life experience can be described by an expression used in the world of computers, "What you see is what you get."

To make maximum progress on your personal path, you need to understand this basic mechanism and how you can use it to free yourself from the imperfections of this world. The only way to rise above limitation is to stop creating limitation. If you allow your conscious mind or subconscious mind to become focused on any imperfect form, you start directing spiritual energy into that form. You direct this energy through your conscious attention or through the beliefs that you allow to accumulate in your subconscious mind. One might say that your conscious and subconscious minds act as a prism which causes the pure light from your spiritual self to be split into different colors. The colors that exit the prism are the result of the condition of the prism itself. If the prism has a flaw, an imperfect color will be the result.

The longer you allow your spiritual energy to flow through an imperfect form, the more tangible, or manifest, the imperfect form becomes. This can most easily be illustrated through the physical body and the process of aging. Medical science has demonstrated that all cells in your body are replaced every seven years. If the cells are constantly renewed, how come the body ages or takes on the imperfections of disease?

If all of your cells were recreated in their original purity, then your body should never age. Your entire body would be renewed every seven years. The fact is that your cells are not recreated in their original purity. The recreation of your cells is a subconscious process that is affected by the beliefs you hold in your conscious and subconscious minds. If you accept the inevitability of old age and imperfection, then new cells will not be whole and pure. They will take on the form of your conscious or subconscious beliefs.

You are a co-creator, and you cannot stop the creative process. Consider the play Hamlet and the eternal question, "To be or not to be?" This question reflects the reality that you can never stop creating. Even if you ignore or deny your creative abilities, energy is still flowing from your spiritual self. That spiritual energy will take on whatever form you allow your mind to dwell upon. Because you cannot empty your mind of thoughts, you cannot stop creating. But once you realize that you are always creating, you can start creating perfect forms instead of continuing to create imperfect forms. To be creating perfection or to be creating imperfection, that is the question!

In the beginning of this book, we considered the idea that deeper understanding is the key to improving your actions. If you apply the inner approach to knowledge, you will attain this deeper understanding, and you will see that it is clearly in your own best interest to stop creating imperfection and start creating perfection. The way to do this is to free your mind of all imperfections in the form of toxic energies, imperfect subconscious computer programs and incorrect beliefs about yourself and life. After you realize the importance of focusing your attention on perfection, the spiritual path will take on an entirely new meaning.

DISCOURSE 10:
Making Peace with God

To fully accept your spiritual identity, you need to make peace with God. Very few people are at peace with God. Most have negative feelings or beliefs that stand between them and their complete acceptance of themselves as God's children.

To make peace with God you must understand the fundamental difference between the reality of God and the beliefs about God that human beings have created throughout the ages. When human beings first lost the direct, inner contact with their spiritual selves, they were no longer able to experience or comprehend the full nature of God. The statement that God created man in his own image and likeness is true as far as the spiritual self and the soul in her original form. However, God did not create the ego or the lower self. Therefore, after human beings lost their contact with God, they created a God in their own image and likeness, or rather in the image and likeness of the ego and the lower self.

God is who God is, regardless of what any human being thinks about God. Because you have the ability to go within and contact your spiritual self, you can know the reality of God. The question is, Are you willing to open your mind and heart so that God can reveal its true identity to you, or will you continue to cling to the human concepts of God that you have come to accept?

Do you want to know the true reality of God, a reality that transcends all words and images found in the world of form? Or are you content with the surrogate images, the idols, that human beings have created? If you are truly willing to open your mind and heart to a direct experience of the nature of God, certain ideas might help you. Let us begin by considering the true nature of God.

The nature of God

When the I AM THAT I AM initiated the impulse that led to the creation of the world of form, the I AM projected its own nature into the world of form. The nature of the I AM is love. Everything in the world of form was created from the same basic substance, namely God's love.

Many people find it difficult to accept that God is love. Once again, the problem is that human beings have created their own concept of love, and it is very far from the reality of divine love. The human concept of love springs from the ego, and the ego sees only the relativity of the material world. Therefore, human love is relative and conditional. People tend to feel that in order to give their love, the object of their love must meet certain conditions.

In contrast to human love, God's love is completely and absolutely unconditional. God's love has no conditions. God's love implies no judgments. God's love has no anger or any of the negative emotions in which human beings so easily indulge. God's love does not want anything in return; it simply gives of itself and continues to give no matter what you do with that gift.

God's love isn't to be confused with God's law. When God gave people free will, God made every person responsible for how he or she uses God's energy. As we will see later, this impersonal law returns all energy to its source. Ultimately, you can never get away with misusing God's energy. However, this impersonal law does not mean that God does not love you; it is a law that God defined to ensure that the world of form will not self-destruct. In fact, God's laws are safety features that prevent you from destroying yourself.

Some people seem to think that if they violate God's laws, God will no longer love them. This idea sprang from the human concept of conditional love. God loved you enough to give you free will and God's love is big enough to see beyond your misuses of that free will. God's love is not affected by your misuses of free will, because God's law makes sure that your misuse can only go so far. When you misuse God's energy, you automatically limit your creative powers. If you continue to do so, you are like a bull tied to a pole. The bull will wind the rope around the pole until the rope is so tight that the bull can no longer move.

God loves you, your soul, with an unconditional and never-ending love. God's love originates directly from the I AM THAT I AM, and it moves through all levels of the world of form to reach you. God is sending that love constantly and unceasingly. Nothing you could possibly do would cause you to lose or turn off God's love. God will send you love no matter what mistakes you have made or what sins you think you have committed.

One of the biggest obstacles that prevents human beings from making peace with God is their creation of the image of an angry, judgmental and conditional God. Let us once again state the basic fact about God's love: You cannot lose God's unconditional love. If you could, God's love would not be truly unconditional, would it? Therefore, no matter what mistakes you have made, God is still sending you undying love. At any moment you can receive the fullness of that love.

Contrary to what many people think, following certain outer laws or rituals is not a condition for receiving God's love. You do not have to do anything to earn God's love, because you permanently earned that love when God created you. Therefore, when it comes to receiving God's love, you only have two options. You can accept God's love or you can reject God's love. Unfortunately, most people choose to reject it.

Stop rejecting God's love!

The biggest problem in the relationship between God and human beings is that so many people have allowed themselves to enter a state of consciousness in which they feel that they are not worthy of receiving God's love. Therefore, they are constantly rejecting God's love and seeking to justify the original decision that caused them to turn their backs on God and reject the love of their spiritual parents.

If you want to move forward on the spiritual path, if you want to attain true inner peace and happiness, you need to realize that your soul is longing to consciously experience the unconditional love of God. Your soul used to experience this love before she fell into a lower state of consciousness. Every longing you feel, every desire you have can ultimately be fulfilled only through God's love. So many people dream of finding the perfect spouse who will fulfill all of their needs. In reality, they are dreaming of the divine romance between their souls and God, between their souls and their spiritual selves.

As you continue to grow on the spiritual path, you will reach a point where the only thing that stands between you and further progress is that you haven't gone back and looked at the original decision that caused you to turn away from God. Once you have done so, you can consciously undo that decision by making a better decision. However, the original decision is at the lowest level of your ego. It is covered over by layers upon layers of decisions made by or influenced by the carnal mind, the lower self and the ego. Therefore, it might take time and effort to uncover the central cause of your separation from God.

Because the ego was created from that original decision, the ego knows that if you were to consciously undo that decision, it would lose all control over you. Therefore, the ego would eventually cease to exist. As a matter of survival, the ego will do anything to prevent you from uncovering and undoing the original decision to turn away from God. The ego will use any means to prevent you from undoing the decision that created it. The ego's survival depends on keeping you from reestablishing your contact with your spiritual self and accepting your divine identity.

Therefore, to reach the very highest step on the spiritual path and win your permanent victory as a free spiritual being, you must expose, outsmart and take command over the ego. Through your conscious understanding and by using the power of your free will, you can separate yourself from the ego and its influence over you.

Is God an angry God?

To be successful on the path, it is necessary to engage in a twofold process. Part of the process has already been described, namely to free your mind from the negative gravitational pull of toxic energies and systematically remove the subconscious computer programs that prevent you from being who you truly are. The other part of the process is to engage in a sincere effort to change your perception of God so that you free yourself from the image of God created by your lower self. Thereby, you can gradually come to know the true reality of God. This is a process that must take place inside yourself. It is an inner walk with God, an inner walk with your higher self. No book can do this for you; a book can only point you in the right direction and help you get started. However, if you are sincere about following this process, your higher self will take you by the hand and lead you all the way home.

You can begin this process by considering the question of whether God is an angry and judgmental God, as he has been portrayed by so many religions. Does this mean that all of these religions are wrong? No, not necessarily. To understand this seeming contradiction, try to step back from the situation and consider a different perspective.

God never rejected you!

God did not create the human ego, and it was not created in accordance with God's original blueprint for your life. The human ego has none of God's qualities, and therefore the human ego has no ultimate reality. If you try to approach God from the consciousness of the human ego, God must reject that approach. God cannot look upon the human ego, because whatever God looks upon becomes magnified by the intense creative power of God. When human beings seek to approach God from a state of consciousness dominated by the ego, God does not even see the approach.

When human beings approach God from the consciousness of the ego, they often feel that God is rejecting them. However, God is not rejecting the individual as a living soul; God is only rejecting the ego, which is not the real person. The problem is that if people are completely identified with their egos, they feel rejected by God.

We have seen that God has many representatives in the form of spiritual beings. In the octave right above the material octave are numerous spiritual beings who have chosen to help human beings move forward on the spiritual path. These spiritual teachers are here to help you find your way back home.

The spiritual teachers are fully aware of the existence of the ego. They are also aware that as long as you identify with the ego, you cannot leave planet Earth behind and return to your home of light in a higher octave. In other words, the human ego is allowed to exist in the material octave, but it will never be allowed to enter into a higher octave. The higher octaves are sealed from any influence of the human ego.

Therefore, the spiritual teachers in a higher octave have a no-tolerance policy towards every aspect and disguise of the lower self. If someone approaches one of these teachers from the lower self, that teacher cannot accept the approach, so the person might feel rejected.

Your spiritual teachers

Following is a little thought experiment to help you imagine what it would be like to be a spiritual teacher assigned to help humankind. Imagine that you are now a spiritual being who is permanently residing in a higher octave and you have earned this position through your hard work. You too were once in embodiment on planet Earth. You walked the spiritual path and you systematically overcame the influence of the lower self and the ego. You have conquered your own ego and therefore God has called you home.

After you ascended from this world, you chose to remain with planet Earth. You chose to engage in the mission of seeking to help the rest of humanity discover and follow the spiritual path. Because you have successfully finished walking that path, you fully understand its requirements. You know that until human beings free themselves from the influence of the ego, they have no chance of ascending to higher octaves. Therefore, your foremost concern is to help people see through the subtle and deceptive influence of the lower self. How can you possibly do this?

Look at planet Earth as you know it today. Look at the many different people you find on Earth and consider that they are in different states of consciousness. Some of them are very dense and it seems almost impossible to reach them with any kind of spiritual message. When you consider the incredible diversity found on the Earth, one thing becomes obvious. If you want to help people discover the spiritual path, one size, one approach, does not fit all. People are so different and they are trapped at so many different levels of consciousness that one religion, one philosophy or one spiritual teaching has no chance of appealing to everyone.

Therefore, you realize that you must take an individual approach. You must look at the individual person and try to assess his or her level of consciousness. Then you need to reach people at the level of consciousness where they are and encourage them come up one single step. Your primary concern is not what it will take to make a person understand everything about the spiritual path. Your primary concern is how any given person can take that very next step that will lead him or her to a deeper understanding of some aspect of life. Once people have achieved that deeper understanding, you can give them further understanding. However, if you try to give them the highest understanding right away, you have no chance of reaching them in their present state of consciousness. They will not understand your message and they might ignore or reject it.

This approach is easy to understand when you compare it to the educational systems found on planet Earth. You cannot teach algebra in kindergarten, because children at that age have no foundation for understanding advanced math. Therefore, you start out slowly by teaching children simple addition and then you gradually give them more advanced lessons. Obviously, the kindergarten curriculum is very limited, and in one sense it might give students a false impression of certain topics. However, you have to start somewhere and allow students to grow at a gradual pace.

Different religions, one purpose

When you begin to understand how the present situation on Earth is perceived by spiritual beings in higher octaves, you can see why this planet has many different religions. Each religion, each spiritual philosophy or teaching, is an attempt to appeal to a certain segment of humankind, to a certain group of souls. Spiritual teachers are trying to bring forth religious teachings that have the capacity to appeal to a certain group of people in their present state of consciousness.

Some people are trapped in such a low and dense state of consciousness that the only way to reach them is to shock them out of that state of mind. They need what one might call spiritual electroshock treatment. That is why some religions seek to awaken people with a very serious message about the dire consequences of people's negative actions. That is why, from time to time, some people have had spiritual experiences that caused them to perceive God as being angry and uncompromising.

The spiritual teachers in higher octaves are not angry with human beings. However, if a very stern message, an uncompromising message, is the only way to awaken people and penetrate the density of the lower consciousness, then a spiritual teacher will take on the role of appearing uncompromising. A spiritual teacher will not spoil the child by sparing the rod. The spiritual teacher knows that until people have been awakened to the need for change, they will make no spiritual progress. After people have been awakened, they have the potential to discover the true inner path. And if people are willing to follow that inner path, they will eventually come to an understanding of the true nature of God, namely unconditional love.

The first task that a spiritual teacher must perform is to awaken the student and help the student realize that he or she needs to change. Human beings have a tendency to become creatures of habit. People often gravitate to a state of consciousness in which they are so blinded by erroneous ideas that they see no need to change or they believe that they could not possibly change.

This is a problem, because God's nature is expansive and ever changing. God is constantly growing and transcending himself. In Western culture, the name of God is commonly translated as "I AM THAT I AM." In reality, the correct translation of the original Hebrew is "I will be who I will be." By making this statement, God has revealed that God is constantly changing and growing. God is the creator and God continues to create. Creation is change, creation is self-transcendence, and God cannot create without transcending itself. Therefore, when people refuse to change, they are out of touch with God's nature, and they are going against one of the fundamental principles of the universe.

Human beings cannot forever remain in the same state of consciousness. They must change and they must grow. In order to grow, people must be shaken out of their sleep, their spiritual sleep, so that they realize the need for growth. When you consider the dense state of consciousness that so many human beings have descended to, you realize that God sometimes has to use drastic measures to make people see the need for change.

Does God punish your sins?
In order to fully make peace with God, you need to consider the concept of punishment. We have already touched upon

this topic but let us take another look. Many religions claim that dramatic events, such as natural disasters or disease, are God's punishment for people's sins. However, is God really punishing human beings? Is it possible that what people see as God's punishment is simply the consequences of their own actions?

Obviously, most people do not understand that they themselves produce outer events. Consider a child who has just learned to walk and is happily walking around the living room. In the living room is a hot wood stove. The parents have attempted to teach the child that the wood stove is hot, yet the child ignores the warning and touches the stove. The child getting burned is not the punishment of some angry God. It is merely the inevitable consequence of the child's actions.

Now consider this in the context of natural laws. If you stand at the edge of a tall building and take a step out into thin air, you will fall to the ground and die. Your death is not an act of punishment perpetrated by an angry God. Your death is the consequence of a natural law. Obviously, you know that the law of gravity exists and therefore you are not likely to step out from the edge of a tall building. Unfortunately, humankind has allowed itself to sink into a state of consciousness in which people no longer know all of God's laws. Therefore, people no longer understand the consequences of their actions.

According to spiritual and natural laws, no human being can escape the consequences of his or her misuse of free will and God's energy. Science cannot yet fully explain these laws, yet most religions describe them in one form or another. Even science opens the possibility that when you send out negative energy, that energy might return to you at some future time. Einstein speculated that if you travel out into the universe and continue in the same direction, you will eventually return to your starting point from the opposite direction. In other words, the time-space continuum forms a closed loop and all energy that is sent into space will return to its source. Eastern religions contain the concept of karma, and even many Western religions contain the concept that a person will reap what he or she has sown.

Consider the teachings about energy that we looked at previously. If you allow toxic energy to accumulate in your personal energy field, that energy can eventually reach such an intensity that it starts affecting the cells of your physical body. This negative effect can manifest itself as various forms of disease, which are a direct consequence of the accumulation of energy. The accumulation of energy is a direct consequence of your state of consciousness, and your state of consciousness is a direct consequence of the choices you have made with your free will. Therefore, it would be naive to reason that the disease is the result of some angry, unseen God who is trying to punish you for your sins. The disease is a direct consequence of your generating negative energy and allowing it to accumulate.

Now take this to a global scale. The entire planet is made from energy. For thousands of years, human beings have continued to accumulate negative energy, not only in their personal energy fields but also in the energy field of the planet. From time to time this energy reaches such an intensity that it has consequences for the planetary body. As your body can become sick, the body of the Earth can also manifest various kinds of disease. When the Earth body gets sick, it manifests as what human beings call natural disasters. Once again, such events are not the punishment of an angry God; rather they are natural consequences of the continued misuse of God's energy.

How can people be awakened?

Let us consider how a group of spiritual teachers could possibly awaken humankind to the need for change. These teachers have designed a universal inner path that can lead a soul back to her true sense of identity. They have even presented this path in many different ways. However, some people have closed their minds so firmly that no spiritual teaching appeals to them. Therefore, they can learn only by reaping the consequences of their own actions. Usually, people do not understand that natural disasters are the consequences of their own actions. Yet because they have refused to look at any spiritual teachings, the spiritual teachers have no way of reaching them. A spiritual teacher cannot violate the free will of the student. Therefore, if the student rejects the teacher, the teacher must leave the student alone. The teacher can only hope that the student will eventually begin to wonder why certain things continue to happen to him or her. The teacher can only hope that the student will eventually develop a desire to avoid negative events and that the student will begin to contemplate that perhaps negative events are somehow tied to his or her own actions.

The purpose of many religious teachings has been to awaken a group of people who were in a very dense state of consciousness. These people needed an image of an angry and judgmental God who was ready to punish them for their sins. As you grow on the path and look beyond these religious doctrines, you can allow your higher self to show you a new understanding of the nature of God. In other words, religious doctrines need not prevent you from gaining a deeper understanding of God or a direct experience of God.

Contemplate the obvious fact that God does not need religion. God already knows who God is. Human beings need religion because they no longer know who God is. But since God is beyond the material universe, God cannot be accurately described through words and images. So humankind's spiritual teachers have never attempted to put forth a teaching that accurately and completely describes God.

The spiritual teachers fully understand that the only way to know God is through a direct inner experience that transcends all words or doctrines. Therefore, the purpose of religion is to help a specific group of people, a group of people living in a particular culture at a particular time, to ascend to a higher level of understanding. So religion is not an end in itself; rather the goal of all true religion is to help you discover the inner path which is independent of all outer doctrines or rituals.

This does not mean that you have to abandon a religion that has meaning to you. It only means that you should see that religion as a stepping stone for your spiritual progress. Religion should not be a cage that entraps your mind and confines you to a particular image of God. If you will contemplate the lives of the saints or sages of any religion, you will discover that these people were all following the inner path, some of them simply did so within the context of a particular outer religion.

Contemplate the first of the Ten Commandments, "Thou shall have no other Gods before me!" What can this commandment tell us about the ideal relationship to God? What if it means that you should never allow anything from this world to come between you and God. If you allow an outer religious teaching, a political philosophy or any other idea to stand between you and a deeper understanding of God, how can you truly know God? If you allow the ego, the lower self or the carnal mind to come between you and your spiritual self, how can you unite with that spiritual self?

The nature of God is unconditional love. To know God's unconditional love is a most satisfying and fulfilling experience. It is in your own best interest to remove all barriers that stand between you and a direct experience of God's love. God has created you in his image and likeness, and you have the capacity to experience the fullness of God's love. If you understand this truth, why would you settle for anything less than God's love? Why would you let anything in this world disturb your inner peace and harmony and thereby prevent you from experiencing God's love? How could any aspect of the material octave possibly be more important or satisfying than experiencing God's love?

Spiritual progress is an inner process between your soul and your spiritual self. If you become attached to outer doctrines or rituals, it will be more difficult to walk that inner path. Spiritual teachings and rituals can be of great help on the path, but they are not an end in themselves. The essence of the path is that your soul frees herself from any attachment to the false sense of identity that is based on the material world. To reclaim her true spiritual identity, the soul must reach beyond all human or material concepts. You must be who you are instead of letting the forces of this world tell you who you should be. You must grow out of the "I should" consciousness and into the "I AM" consciousness.

DISCOURSE 11:
Opposition from Within

The point that will be explained in this discourse is a point that has tripped up and confused numerous seekers on the spiritual path. Therefore, apply the inner approach to knowledge and allow your higher self to give you a direct inner understanding of the following ideas.

We have seen that the very essence of the spiritual path is that your soul must undo her false sense of identity and rebuild her true spiritual identity. The soul must free herself from the sense of identity that is based on the ego and the lower self and reclaim the true spiritual identity that is based on the higher self and the spiritual self. To complete this process, the soul needs to develop her ability and willingness to discern between truth and untruth, reality and unreality. Unreality is that which is based on the ego, the lower self, the carnal mind and any false concept originating in the material octave. Reality is that which is based on God, the emissaries of God, your spiritual self and true concepts originating in a higher octave.

The essence of the path is to reach for a deeper understanding, which can only come from higher octaves. Many of the spiritual and religious teachings found on this planet contain elements of truth, yet to fully grasp truth you must go beyond any outer expression of it. Truth is not a matter of words and ideas; truth is a matter of vibration. Truth is a matter of the light of God that never fails. By calling forth that light, you can learn to recognize what is of the light and what is not of the light. Then, when your soul has developed the ability to discern between light and darkness, your soul can make a decision to choose the light, to choose life.

We have seen that your higher self acts as a spiritual teacher who will give you understanding. Likewise, many spiritual teachers in higher octaves will help you attain greater understanding. Many of these teachers are known as saints and spiritual leaders. They include Jesus, Gautama Buddha, Krishna, Lao-tzu, Confucius, Mother Mary, Saint Francis, El Morya, Kuthumi, Kuan Yin, Saint Germain and many others. While such spiritual teachers can give you invaluable assistance on the path, they cannot and will not make decisions for you. For each step you take on the spiritual path, you must make a decision to let go of some aspect of the lower self and the ego. This is a decision that you and you alone must make.

In the end, you cannot make this decision as long as you identify with the ego or think that the ego is somehow necessary. We have seen that the soul created the ego as a substitute for the spiritual self. Therefore, the soul is accustomed to thinking that the ego is necessary and that she could not live without the ego. The soul thinks that she would be alone and incomplete without the ego, but this is an illusion. In reality, the soul can only attain wholeness by reuniting with the spiritual self. To reunite with the spiritual self, the soul must free herself from the illusions of the ego. The soul must allow the ego to die!

You don't need the ego

Throughout the ages, many seekers have found the inner path and have made great spiritual progress. Yet all seekers inevitably come to a point where they are faced with the need to let go of the ego. If a person has not understood or accepted the unreality of the ego, he or she may not be willing to let go of it. Many souls have remained attached to some aspect of the ego, and therefore their spiritual progress has come to an abrupt halt. Let it be stated clearly that you cannot take the final steps on the spiritual path without letting go of the ego! There are no two ways about this, and there is no possibility of a compromise.

Many spiritual seekers, even some so-called spiritual teachers, believe that they can somehow refine or raise the ego. They think that if only they can perfect the ego, it will become acceptable in the eyes of God. Therefore, they engage in a path of seeking to justify, refine and perfect the human ego. This path is not the true spiritual path. It is "the way that seems right unto a man, but the end thereof is the way of death." This false path leads to the death of the soul instead of the death of the ego.

When all is said and done, when all unreality is stripped away, it all boils down to this: the ego must die so that the soul can live forever in the light of God! If the soul does not let go of the ego, the soul will eventually die. Then the ego will die with it because the ego has no light of its own. The ego does not understand this, and it will desperately seek to maintain its stranglehold on the soul. Therefore, it is up to the soul to override the ego's misguided survival instinct.

A soul does not have an eternity to decide that it wants to come back home. God has great mercy upon souls and is willing to help them in any way possible. Yet the consequence of having free will is that you cannot postpone the choice forever. You cannot choose not to make choices. Everything in the material universe is temporary and transient. At some point, you must choose which master you want to serve—the ego or the spiritual self. If you were able to postpone this choice forever, you really would not have freedom of choice.

This explanation may seem unduly strict and absolute. But as the one aspect that will make or break your progress on the spiritual path, you need to be aware of what is at stake. The fact is that you cannot serve two masters. You cannot hold on to and seek to perfect or justify the ego and at the same time seek to unify with your spiritual self. Therefore, it is wise to let go of all desire for a compromise.

We earlier discussed how even God must make certain choices. God can create a round planet or God can create a flat planet. However, God cannot create a planet that is both round and flat at the same time, because the two concepts are mutually exclusive. When you choose one option, you cannot simultaneously choose another option. You can have the darkness of the ego or you can have the light of the spiritual self, but you cannot take the darkness of the ego with you into the octaves of light. Light and darkness do not coexist, because darkness is the absence of light.

The path is a gradual process

While you walk the spiritual path, you go through a transition period in which you have both light and darkness in your consciousness. In other words, you do not suddenly walk out of the darkness and into the light.

You start by going through a stage in which you gradually let go of certain elements of the ego and gradually accept certain elements of the higher self. This was explained by Saint Paul when he said, "I die daily." What he meant was that a part of his ego and lower self died every day. He also stated that he was "putting off the old man and putting on the new man." In other words, while he was gradually letting go of elements of the ego, he was gradually accepting and putting on his true spiritual identity. This is a process that takes place step-by-step, which is why it is often described as a path. The soul cannot suddenly shift her identity away from the ego and towards the spiritual self. An attempt to do so could throw that soul into an identity crisis that might cause insanity.

The only way to take a step forward on the path is by consciously and willingly letting go of some aspect of the ego and accepting the reality of your spiritual self. Trying to accept the spiritual self without letting go of the ego will put your soul at an impasse, or stalemate. Your soul will make no progress until that stalemate is broken, and this must be done by accepting that the ego is unreal and that it must go.

The spiritual path is a process whereby you will gradually become aware of certain elements of the ego. The way to make swifter progress is to realize that whenever you come to identify something as the ego, that something must go. If you try to ignore it, explain it away, justify it or somehow think that you can perfect it, you will slow down your progress on the path. The way to make swifter progress is to say, "Okay, I see that this is unreal and part of the ego. I am joyfully and lovingly surrendering this to God and allowing God to take it away from me. I am also allowing my higher self to fill the vacuum, and I accept my true, divine identity instead of this particular aspect of my human identity." If you will make a commitment to do this, you can make unlimited progress on the spiritual path.

To grow or not to grow

The soul has been identified with the ego for so long that she has become quite comfortable in her false sense of identity. Consequently, it will sometimes be very unpleasant and uncomfortable for the soul to see and acknowledge a particular aspect of the ego. The realization that a particular trait or belief is of the ego can be a rude awakening, a hitting-the-concrete experience.

If the soul is attached to her false sense of identity, it can be very painful for the soul to separate herself out from that sense of identity. If the soul were to remain where she was comfortable, she could not possibly make any spiritual progress. Therefore, the soul needs to choose between comfortability and growth.

Another way to describe the path is in terms of wholeness. Because the soul has been separated from the spiritual self, she feels unwhole. Consequently, the most basic need of the soul is to reestablish the wholeness that she once knew. Because the soul has lost contact with the spiritual self, she has sought to attain wholeness in the material world. But this is an impossible quest that can never be fulfilled. Yet if the soul does not realize this, she will continue to cling to the ego. After all, the ego does give the soul a sense of not being alone.

Seeking to find wholeness in the material world leads to attachment to certain elements of this transient realm. The soul thinks that the key to wholeness is to possess some aspect of the material world. So the soul engages in a quest to acquire or keep something that it deems of value. Attachment to anything that is transient will inevitably lead to suffering, for the soul either fears that she can never attain what she does not have or that she can lose what she does have.

As a result of feeling unwhole and trying to find wholeness in an unwhole world, the soul often finds herself in a situation where everything seems to cause pain. The soul's attachment to the things of this world also causes the soul disappointment and pain. On top of this, the only way to overcome these two forms of pain is to let go of the ego, but because the soul is attached to the ego, that also causes pain.

So some people feel that life is like walking on broken glass; every step causes pain and the soul sees no way out.

In reality, the soul does have a way out. By understanding the situation, the soul can consciously choose to let go of her attachment to the material world and the ego. Pain is caused by one thing and one thing only, namely an emotional attachment to a false sense of identity, an identity based on the ego and the material world. By consciously letting go of this attachment, the pain will vanish into thin air.

In the beginning, letting go of your false sense of identity might cause you some pain. However, the pain of growth is only as severe as you make it. The intensity of the pain is in direct proportion to the intensity of your identification with and attachment to a particular element of the ego and the lower self. The more you can let go of that sense of identity and attachment, the easier and less painful it will be to let go of the ego itself. If you will truly open your heart to experience the unconditional love of God, that love will literally consume the pain of letting go of what is unreal.

Your higher self and your spiritual teachers are completely committed to your spiritual growth. They will not compromise that growth by indulging your ego. Therefore, they will not spare you the pain of a rude awakening if that awakening can propel you forward on the path. This does not mean that your spiritual teachers are insensitive or that they want you to experience pain. What it does mean is that they will never do you the disservice of indulging the unreality of the ego.

If you ask your higher self or a spiritual teacher for help and direction on the path, you might get a rude awakening. If you identify with a particular aspect of the ego, you might feel that you are being hurt or rejected by the teacher. In reality, the teacher never rejects you, the soul. However, the teacher will reject the ego and any attempt by your soul to justify or perfect the ego. Your soul is like the phoenix bird that must rise from the ashes of your lower self, but your soul can only rise when the lower self is consumed by the spiritual fires of truth and reality. However, as always, the key element is your free will. You must, consciously and willingly, let go of the ego.

The keys to letting go of the ego

What are the keys to letting go of the ego, the lower self, the carnal mind and all attachment to the things of this world? The first key is to fully understand and practice forgiveness.

Throughout the ages, most people have completely misunderstood the nature and importance of forgiveness. Many have felt that if they have been harmed by another person, then it is necessary to hold on to negative feelings towards that person. People feel that if they forgive others, they somehow let them off the hook. It seems that many people think that by not forgiving another person, they are somehow holding that person responsible for his or her actions.

In reality, the laws of God, which return all misqualified energy to its source, will hold every person responsible for his or her actions. "Vengeance is mine says the Lord, I will repay!" Therefore, you need never be concerned about holding another person responsible. By setting up a completely impersonal law, God has already made sure that ultimately no human being can escape the responsibility for his or her actions.

In reality, forgiving another person is not letting that person off the hook. Forgiving another person is letting yourself off the hook. Let us consider why forgiveness is enlightened self-interest.

If someone harms you and you continue to hold negative feelings towards that person, you will misqualify energy. Some of that energy will be stored in your personal energy field. Some of it will be sent to the other person, and the universe will eventually return it to your own doorstep. In many cases, two people have created a destructive, downward spiral between them. This spiral might have started with a wrongful act committed by one person. Yet if the second person uses that act as an excuse to also misqualify the pure energies of God, then both of them are responsible for creating a negative spiral. This is especially dangerous if they seek revenge against each other.

Before they know it, they are sucked into a negative spiral which they no longer have the power to break. This is how family feuds and wars between nations have started.

If you are serious about spiritual growth, you simply cannot afford to start or maintain such negative spirals. When a negative spiral has been created in one of your relationships, someone has to break it and that someone should be the person who is most concerned with his or her own spiritual growth. If you are reading this book, that person is you. Therefore, it is in your own best interest to break off any negative spirals you have with other people.

If someone harms you and you do not forgive that person, then you create a tie, a bond of misqualified energy, between yourself and that person. You become attached to that person, and, as we have discussed, all attachment leads to pain. Ask yourself this question, "If someone has harmed me, why on Earth would I want to remain attached to that person?" Doing so is obviously not in your own best interest. You do not want to be attached to that person; you want to move on in your spiritual unfoldment. You want to be free of negative people!

When you consider the reasons for forgiving, you begin to understand why so many spiritual teachers have talked about the importance of forgiveness. Jesus told people to forgive seventy times seven, because he fully understood the importance of forgiveness. Do you think that the spiritual beings in higher octaves go around holding grudges against each other? In Heaven, you cannot find nonforgiveness; therefore your soul cannot take her nonforgiveness into the octaves of light. Nonforgiveness can become a millstone around the neck of your soul. Therefore you must realize that forgiving someone else is giving your soul freedom to put on the garments of light.

Forgiveness includes the following actions:

- Forgive all people who have ever harmed you.

- Forgive yourself for harming any other part of life.

- Forgive your soul for identifying with the ego and accepting the manipulation and lies of the ego.

- Forgive God for anything your soul has ever imagined that God has done against you.

- Forgive God for setting up a law that forces you to face the consequences of your own wrong choices.

- Forgive God for giving you free will and thereby giving you the potential to fall.

- Forgive God for creating you, so you can accept life as a true gift instead of looking at it as something that was forced upon you.

Judge not

Jesus made the statement, "Judge not, lest you be judged." The reason it is so important not to judge is that all human judgments spring from the ego and its attempts to gain recognition. The ego thinks that if it can make someone else look bad, then it will somehow look better. It wants to elevate itself by tearing down others.

The ego can only see the relativity of the material universe, so it can never make righteous judgments. Since all of the ego's judgments are relative, it can always find a reason to judge and criticize. If you look at other people through the relativity of the ego, you can always interpret a situation in a negative way. Your ego is constantly looking for ways to criticize and judge, and it is always seeking to make you accept its judgments. If you allow yourself to be pulled into the ego's game of playing the judge, you will limit your spiritual growth in the following ways:

- You will misqualify energy and it will eventually come back to haunt you.

- You will violate one of the basic laws of God by harming other people. Thoughts can be powerful, and you have probably experienced that it can be extremely unpleasant to have someone else hold a negative attitude towards you. You are constantly creating, and if you allow yourself to focus on a negative image of another person, you are using your creative abilities against that person's free will. The more spiritual energy you allow to flow into such a negative matrix, the greater the risk that the energy will affect the other person. And you will be held responsible for that misuse of God's energy.

- Your ego will never stop judging, and if you go along with it, you can continue this game for an indefinite period of time. Unfortunately, you cannot maintain a judgmental attitude and at the same time make spiritual progress. The two are mutually exclusive.

- As you do unto others, you do unto yourself. That is why Jesus made his famous statement about doing unto others as you want them to do unto you. If you have a judgmental and critical attitude towards others, you are subconsciously judging and criticizing yourself. Therefore, you are holding a negative image of yourself and you are allowing spiritual energy to flow into that matrix. Eventually the energy will reach a critical mass and start affecting your life. The results are never beneficial.

- If you go along with the ego's judgments, you must obviously think that it is necessary or beneficial to judge people. Therefore, you will unwittingly accept the ego's judgments of yourself. Because the ego does not want you to escape its control, it will not judge your spiritual progress in a favorable manner. If you accept the ego's judgment of your spiritual progress, you will expose yourself to much unnecessary doubt, fear and emotional pain. That is why judgmental people rarely manage to follow the true spiritual path. They often think they are far better than others, and they might actually believe they are especially spiritual because of the outer things they have done. However, this is only the way that seems right unto a man, but it is unacceptable in the eyes of God.

The true goal of the spiritual path is to overcome the false identity that makes you feel like a material, limited and mortal being. If you go along with the ego's tendency to judge yourself and others, you cannot free yourself from this pseudo identity. In fact, the more you judge, the more you attach yourself to your imperfect sense of identity. If you are serious about spiritual progress, you must realize that a judgmental and critical attitude is a huge liability that you simply cannot afford.

You must also realize that divine judgment is very different from human judgment. God judges righteous judgments, because God evaluates what is of the light and what is not of the light. However, God never condemns you for making a mistake. God is not concerned about making you feel like a miserable sinner. God wants you to learn from your mistakes and use them as stepping stones for taking another step closer to home. The last thing God wants to do is to discourage you from walking the path. Therefore, God's judgment is actually an attempt to make you see what is of the light and what is not of the light.

Because God is unconditional love, God's judgments are never critical or condemning. God divides the real from the unreal so that you have a better foundation for choosing whom you will serve. God might condemn an act but God never condemns a person, and you should do the same. It is best to follow your higher self and avoid wasting energy by judging yourself or others.

The magnet of divine love

The next key to letting go of the ego is loving something more than the ego. Your soul cannot exist in a vacuum; she cannot let go of the ego without having something that can replace the ego. If you study the lives of many of the saints and spiritual people from the past, you will see that they faced many trials and tribulations. What carried them through difficult times was that they had a sincere and deep love for God or for a spiritual being, such as Jesus or the Buddha.

In today's materialistic society, many people grow up without developing a deep love for God or for a spiritual figure. This is one of the consequences of living in a materialistic and scientific age. However, you will make much swifter progress on the spiritual path if you will open your heart and seek to develop a deep and sincere love for something that is above and beyond your ego. If loving God seems too abstract, then seek to find some religious figure, be it Jesus, Buddha or another spiritual figure. If this seems difficult, then focus your attention on your higher self or your spiritual self and seek to develop a love for that part of your own being. If even this is too hard, then seek to love another human being, such as a child or spouse, more than your ego.

As is the case with forgiveness, many people have misunderstood the concept of love. As stated earlier, God's love is not conditional. True love is not possessive, and it does not know boundaries or conditions. Therefore, true love is a magnet that attracts your soul.

Because your soul has become accustomed to the ego, your soul fears that by letting go of the ego she will find herself in a vacuum. Contemplate the saying that Perfect Love Casts Out All Fear. The only way that your soul can overcome her fear of losing the ego is by developing a love for something that is above the ego. Your soul must allow that love to form a magnet so strong that it pulls the soul out of the grips of the ego.

Love is the glue that holds the universe together. Love is the glue that keeps your soul tethered to your spiritual self. Your spiritual self has an undying love for your soul, but your soul may have forgotten that love. If so, you can rekindle that love by your sincere effort. When you open your heart to the love of your spiritual self, that love will flow into your soul. To escape the downward gravitational pull of the ego, your soul must be pulled up by a force that is stronger than the energies of this world. That force is the divine love coming from your spiritual self. If your soul rejects that love, she will remain stuck in the muddled energies of the ego. If your soul accepts that love, she can cross over the bridge formed by divine love.

Your higher self and your spiritual teachers exist only to assist you on your personal path. They would do anything to help you, yet they are limited by the means of communication between this world and the worlds above it. The greatest desire of your spiritual teachers is to somehow communicate to you the intense love that God has for your soul. Were you to experience and accept that love, the pain of letting go of the ego would seem so insignificant that you would quickly turn away from the unreality of the lower self and cast yourself into the loving embrace of your spiritual self. No earthly pain could ever be as intense as the love of God. Therefore, no sacrifice of the lower self would ever be too great if you knew that the reward was the unlimited and unconditional love of God. Contemplate that love. Open your heart to that love.

It is truly the Father's good pleasure to give you the kingdom of unconditional love. You do not have to earn that love. You only have to open your heart and accept that you are worthy to receive it. Open your heart, and God will pour out such a measure of love that there shall not be room enough in your heart to receive all of it. Your heart will be the cup that overflows with divine love, and that love will flow into the world and inspire other people to follow the spiritual path. Thereby your heart will become the open door for divine love, the open door which no ego can shut.

DISCOURSE 12:
Opposition from Without

Your ego, lower self and carnal mind form an inner force that opposes your progress. Unfortunately, you will also encounter outside forces that seek to oppose your growth. Many spiritually interested people are reluctant to consider the existence of dark forces or the concept of evil. This is understandable yet unwise.

Both materialistic scientists and some religious people spend vast amounts of energy arguing that evil does not exist, and there is a psychological mechanism behind this denial. The soul, as a matter of emotional survival, cannot and will not recognize the existence of a danger from which she believes she has no protection. If the soul were to acknowledge the existence of a danger from which she could not be defended, she would be paralyzed with fear. Therefore, at certain levels of the path, it can be necessary for the soul to deny the existence of evil. One might say that doing so is the lesser of two evils. However, as the soul begins to know and experience the inner light, she must transcend all fear of dark forces. A state of consciousness dominated by fear can never promote spiritual growth.

Your soul-memory

Deep within your soul is the memory of your spiritual origin. Your soul was born in a world where there was no darkness and no evil. Because your soul feels that evil should not exist, she can be reluctant to recognize that there is darkness in this world. However, as you grow in stature on the path, you will gradually come to rely upon your higher self or upon certain spiritual beings that act as your teachers. Then you will realize that the forces of darkness are no match for the forces of light because God's light and God's emissaries can protect you from any energy or force in this world.

Because most people did not grow up with an understanding of negative energy or evil forces, they tend to respond with fear when they hear about such forces. However, the first step towards overcoming any problem is to recognize the existence of the problem. With our present understanding of energy, it becomes easy to see that evil forces are created from the energies of the material world. Therefore, you can defend yourself from all such forces by invoking the spiritual light of a higher octave.

To build your spiritual defense, it might help to consider the existence of spiritual beings who are assigned specifically to protect your faith and your progress on the path. One of the spiritual beings assigned to protect you from darkness is Archangel Michael. Another is Lord Shiva, who serves as the destroyer of all that is unreal. Although these beings have become known through a particular religion, a spiritual being can never be confined to any outer doctrine. Therefore, seeking the protection of Shiva does not make you a Hindu any more than seeking the protection of Michael makes you a Jew or a Christian. These spiritual beings unconditionally protect any seeker on the path.

However, spiritual beings cannot protect you against your free will. In the section that explains why prayer isn't always answered, we talked about the fact that your subconscious computer programs can neutralize a conscious prayer. This also applies when you call to a spiritual being for protection. If you have some subconscious belief or attachment, it might prevent a spiritual being from giving you full protection. Therefore, as you begin to remove such subconscious programs, you will experience a greater degree of spiritual protection and you will begin to trust that Archangel Michael can protect you from all darkness.

If you were to experience the dedication of Archangel Michael or Lord Shiva, you would know that they are absolutely committed to their job. They have a no-nonsense, no-compromise attitude towards the forces of darkness that reside in this world. They can protect you from all darkness, and they will protect you from all darkness if you will only invite them to do so. You can invoke this protection through a silent prayer or a spoken affirmation.

As you grow on the path, you will become more sensitive to negative energy and you will begin to recognize when you are being attacked by dark forces. When you experience negative energy, make the call to Archangel Michael or Shiva. You can use affirmations as described in part one, and you will gain a greater effect by speaking the affirmations aloud. Start by giving a short invocation and describe the energy you feel. Then, give one or several of the following affirmations. When you are finished, seal your affirmation as described in part one.

One technique is to repeat the name Shiva 9, 33 or 144 times. Or you can keep repeating the name until you no longer feel any negative energy.

Following are a few affirmations to invoke the protection of Archangel Michael. However, you can use the name Lord Shiva or the name of another religious figure instead of Archangel Michael.

Archangel Michael, protect me from all imperfect energies!

Archangel Michael, protect me from all evil!

Archangel Michael, bind all evil forces attacking my soul!

Archangel Michael, bind my ego, my carnal mind and my lower self!

Archangel Michael, cut me free from all imperfect energies!

Archangel Michael, consume all imperfect energies in my consciousness!

There are other ways to invoke the protection of spiritual beings, and you can find specific rituals in many religious and spiritual teachings. You can also find a large selection at www.askrealjesus.com..

Overcoming your fear of dark forces

One aspect of the path is contemplating and resolving your relationship to God. You also need to recognize the existence of forces that will aggressively seek to prevent you from making progress on the path. You must overcome all fear of dark forces so that you can permanently escape their influence. These forces have several reasons for trying to prevent your spiritual progress:

- They do not want you to become an electrode for the light of God to shine forth in this world.

- They do not want you to escape from the deception they have created, a deception which makes so many people believe that this world is separated from God.

- Dark forces are cut off from God and from God's light. Without God's light, nothing has permanence, nothing has life. Beings who have completely turned away from God cannot receive God's light directly. They could do so if they were willing to engage in the spiritual path. However, because of pride and other negative emotions, they are not willing to walk the inner path.

- Dark forces can only continue to exist by stealing light from those who have not yet extinguished the direct contact to their spiritual selves. As you advance on the path, you will carry more light. Therefore, dark forces will have a greater incentive to steal that light from you.

The modus operandi of dark forces

The material octave has become a temporary abode for certain dark forces. These forces chose to rebel against God, the laws of God and the vision of God. Because of this rebellion, they could no longer remain in the higher octaves. Instead, they were sent to the material octave and here they were given another opportunity to choose between light and darkness.

In their anger and arrogance, these forces have attempted to create a planetary illusion which states that God does not exist or that this world is separated from God. They are constantly trying to make every human being accept the idea that people are cut off from God and that God has no way to act in this world.

When you have a deeper understanding of the importance of free will, you can see through the illusion created by dark forces. God does indeed have a way to act in this world. Yet because God has given human beings free will, God can only act in this world when people, such as yourself, make the choice to allow God to act through them.

For thousands of years, dark forces have attempted to create and cement the illusion that human beings do not have the capacity to be instruments for God's light. These forces would have you believe that it is blasphemy to consider yourself as a son or daughter of God. They would have you believe that only very special people, such as Jesus, have the capacity to act as God's emissaries on Earth. And because Jesus is now gone, no one can do what he did. They will do anything to prevent you from following in the footsteps of a spiritual teacher, such as Jesus. They would have you subscribe to the popular illusion that Jesus was an exception and that no other person can be the open door for God to act in this octave.

To free yourself from this illusion, contemplate the statements, "The works that I do shall you do also, and greater works shall you do!" and "Let that mind be in you which was also in Christ Jesus!" By applying the inner approach to knowledge, you will see that you too have the capacity to be an instrument for God's light. You too can be the open door which no material forces can shut.

Why are the dark forces so intent on preventing God's light from entering this world through the hearts and minds of human beings? Because they will do anything to maintain the illusion that this world is separated from God. In reality, the dark forces are attempting to do something that simply cannot be done. We have seen that everything was created from God's light. Without God's light, nothing has permanence. If the dark forces were successful in completely shutting out God's light, this world would immediately cease to exist and so would the dark forces themselves. This is similar to the fact that if your soul were to die, your ego would die with her. The ego does not see this because it suffers from spiritual blindness, and so do all dark forces. Therefore, the dark forces do not see that they are, in reality, committing spiritual suicide by seeking to kill the goose that lays the golden eggs of light.

As you begin to contemplate these concepts, you will realize that it is up to you, and other people who are open to the inner path, to reverse the downward spiral created by dark forces. It should not be difficult to see that civilization has a certain propensity towards self-destruction. To gain a better understanding of this problem, we can once again look to the field of science.

Why evil is temporary

One of the fundamental laws of physics is the second law of thermodynamics. This law states that in a closed system, entropy will increase. The dark forces are attempting to turn planet Earth into a closed system that does not receive any energy or truth from God. If they could make all human beings believe in their illusions, then people might completely cut off the connection to their spiritual selves. Were this to happen, planet Earth might indeed become a closed system that would not receive any ideas or energy from higher octaves. Then human civilization would quickly self-destruct.

When you look at the current state of affairs on this planet, you see that although the process is by no means complete, the dark forces have attained a certain measure of success. Many people, especially in Western civilization, seem to believe that they are cut off from God or that God does not exist. This widespread illusion has caused a decrease in the stream of spiritual light, and Western civilization has entered a spiral of decay and self-destruction. The fact is that society has become subject to the second law of thermodynamics. When a civilization cuts itself off from the truth and energy of God, then entropy and disorder will inevitably increase. The civilization will continue to sink further and further into self-destruction unless a critical mass of people choose to turn the situation around by making themselves the open door through which God can bring light and enlightened ideas.

You have the potential to be an instrument for the forces of light, an instrument that can help turn around the downward course of civilization. Indeed, this might be the main reason why your soul chose to descend to planet Earth. Apply the inner approach to knowledge and allow your higher self to show you if this does indeed apply to you. If so, embrace this mission and fulfill it in full measure.

Lead all people away from temptation

We are discussing the subject of dark forces because, once again, being forewarned is being forearmed. You will find it difficult to walk the spiritual path if you do not realize the existence of forces who are trying to prevent your progress. If you are not aware of these forces, you will encounter much opposition on the path and you will be unable to understand where it comes from. Once you understand that the opposition comes from forces who are deliberately and aggressively trying to prevent your progress, it becomes much easier to protect yourself.

In contemplating the existence of dark forces, it is extremely important for you not to put too much attention on them. First of all, never allow yourself to enter into a vibration of fear. You do not need to fear evil, because from a higher viewpoint evil has no reality and no permanence. Only that which is created in accordance with the spiritual and natural laws of God can attain permanence. Because dark forces keep turning away from God, they are doomed to a temporary existence.

Evil has no power beyond what it receives from human beings. Evil has no reality. It is an illusion and it only appears to have power in this world. However, if you choose to give power to evil, then evil can influence you on a temporary basis. Once again, the forces of light cannot protect you if you choose to give power to evil forces. Then the forces of light must stand back and wait until you make a better choice and ask for their protection.

The topic of evil can be depressing and even boring. Yet it must be discussed if you are to attain ultimate success on the spiritual path. At every point on your spiritual path, you will be confronted with forces (from within or without) that will seek to prevent your progress. Therefore, you will be tempted by evil in various ways. In this context, you can find much guidance and inspiration in the lives of other people who have walked the spiritual path. Consider very carefully the account of how Jesus was tempted by the Devil. Consider also the story of Gautama Buddha who, at the brink of entering nirvana (meaning that he was at the very last step of the spiritual path), was attacked by the demons of Mara, who sought to tempt him into somehow reacting to their appearances.

Dark forces will seek to tempt you in many subtle and clever ways. They will seek to steal your light by making you misqualify that light through inharmonious thoughts, feelings and actions. They will seek to make you believe in all kinds of illusions. But first of all, they will seek to prevent you from letting go of your attachments to your ego, your lower self or any aspect of the material world.

Consider the story of the Garden of Eden. Eve represents the soul, which is the feminine polarity of your being as the spiritual self is the masculine polarity. Why did the soul fall for the temptation presented by the Serpent? Because of doubt. At first, the soul believed that if she ate of the fruit, she would die. The Serpent inserted the element of doubt by the statement that the soul would not "surely" die. Once the soul was in the claws of doubt, she was quickly overcome by temptation. Your soul still faces the enemy of doubt, and you must overcome it every time you take another step on the path. You can only do so by reaching for a deeper understanding, an understanding that comes through your higher self. When you have that clarity, you can avoid the enemy of doubt.

Learn by example

It can be a great help and inspiration to consider how your spiritual brothers and sisters resisted the temptations of evil. The evil forces were seeking to make Jesus and Buddha react to their temptations or appearances. If evil forces had managed to make Jesus or Buddha engage in anger, fear, doubt or any other negative emotion, the evil forces would have won a temporary victory. You too will be tempted by the appearances and deceptions of evil. Certain forces will seek to manipulate you into engaging in negative feelings, thoughts or actions.

What enabled Jesus and Gautama to withstand the temptations of evil? These spiritual exemplars walked the very same inner path that you are walking. They too had to overcome the ego, the lower self and the carnal mind. The Christ and the Buddha had systematically overcome the negative effects of this enemy within. These spiritual teachers, and many others, were meant to serve as examples to show you the path that you too can follow. Because of the intense idolatry that has been built around such teachers, you can easily fall into the trap of thinking that they were somehow special.

Thereby you come to think that their examples do not apply to you and that you are so far beneath them that you could not possibly reach the same level of attainment.

Jesus and Buddha were indeed special. They were sons of God, even as you are a son or daughter of God. Each of them had a unique individuality, just as you have a unique individuality. They might have had greater attainment on the spiritual path than you have, yet it remains a fact that you, too, can follow the inner path and you, too, can win the final victory over the forces of this world.

The very key element that allowed the Christ and the Buddha to withstand the temptations of evil can be expressed in this sentence, "The prince of this world comes and has nothing in me!" Because Jesus and Gautama had overcome the ego, the lower self and the carnal mind, the forces of this world had nothing whereby they could gain control over them. Jesus had no element of the ego left through which the Devil could tempt him. The Buddha had no element of the ego through which the forces of Mara could make him react to their appearances.

Because they had overcome the ego, Jesus and Gautama were not attached to the appearances of this world. They had their eyes fixed on their spiritual selves, and they clearly saw that no matter what appearances might exist in this world, these appearances were ultimately unreal and impermanent. Because such appearances are not created in accord with the laws of God, they have no reality and no power of their own. They only have the power which human beings give them. And if you do not give them energy and attention, they have no power over you.

Evil can only influence you through the power which you give to it. You give it power through the ego, the lower self and the carnal mind. If you free yourself from these enemies within, the enemy without can no longer touch you.

Opposition from Without

Overcoming the ego is the soul's ultimate escape and protection. Nonattachment is the key to victory.

One might say that innocence is the soul's best defense, but it cannot be blind innocence. You must be wise as a serpent (so that you can see through the temptations of evil), and you must be harmless as a dove (so that you can avoid reacting to evil). Consider the idea that to overcome evil it is not necessary to fight evil in an outer sense. To overcome evil on a personal level, you must become nonattached to its illusory appearances. You have overcome evil when it no longer has any way to tempt your soul, and you can achieve that through nonattachment to the things of this world.

This does not mean that you should be passive towards the forces of evil. However, if you seek to fight evil on its terms, you will become attached to it. Thus, even if you win a battle, the forces of evil will win the war. The only way to win over evil is to let God and the emissaries of God fight the battle for you. You can make yourself the instrument of bringing forth God's light and truth, but you must recognize that God is acting through you. If you become personally involved in the fight against evil, if you are attached to the outcome or think that it is you who are fighting evil, you will not assist God in removing these forces from the planet. Instead, you will only add to the pool of misqualified energy that keeps evil alive. Therefore, when you join the fight against evil, you must always seek to do what you know is right (through the inner approach to knowledge) and then be nonattached to the outcome.

DISCOURSE 13:
Discovering Your True Identity

As you grow on the path, you will begin to get a clearer picture of who you are and why you are here on Earth. The answer to the riddle of identity has two parts. One part is individual, and you must receive that answer through your higher self. However, we can now formulate a general answer to the question of your true identity and your reason for being.

You are a son or daughter of God. Your lifestream, meaning your soul and your spiritual self, is the offspring of two divine parents who reside in a higher octave. These parents form a perfect, divine polarity, and through their spiritual union your lifestream was created.

You are here on Earth because you chose to come here. You might have made that choice for one or more of the following reasons:

- Your soul wanted to experience what it was like to see life from the perspective of the material octave and the human body.

- You desired to express your unique individuality, your unique spiritual flame, in the material universe.

- You desired to bring the light of God into the darkness and density of this octave.

- You desired to help rescue some of the souls who are stuck in the material world.

Contemplate the idea that you have a mission, a reason for being here on Earth. In a general sense, that reason is to bring God's light. You have the capacity to become the open door through which God can bring light into this darkened world. By choosing to open your soul, heart and consciousness to the light of God, you can become an electrode that can help raise the consciousness of humankind as a whole. Jesus said, "If I be lifted up, I will draw all men unto me." Likewise, if one person raises his or her consciousness, it will help raise the consciousness of every human being on the planet.

Beyond this general mission, you have a personal mission to fulfill. That mission is to bring forth your unique spiritual flame. As you remove the dense layers of the lower self and the ego, your true spiritual identity will begin to shine through. At first, you will see it "through a glass darkly." But as you keep on removing the layers of unreality that surround your soul, your true spiritual flame will begin to shine more brightly.

When your lifestream was created by your spiritual parents, it was created to express one of the qualities of God. Everything in your life is shaped by your God-quality. Even your ego is created from the relative version of your God-quality, and the ego is using this relative quality to ensnare your soul.

The Fall revisited

Let us return to the situation in the Garden of Eden. Your soul was in the Garden to learn how to express her God-quality through a physical body. During this learning process, your soul became impatient. This is not necessarily a negative quality, and it shows zest, eagerness and curiosity, which are natural qualities of the soul. Yet because your soul had not attained the correct balance, you made the decision to eat the forbidden fruit. But remember that the cause of the soul's fall was not the decision to eat the forbidden fruit. The real cause of the Fall was that the soul, after eating the fruit, decided to hide from her spiritual teacher. It was this decision that caused the soul to fall into the "outer darkness" of the material world.

The forbidden fruit represents the knowledge of relative good and evil. Before your soul partook of the forbidden fruit, she knew only her particular God-quality. For example, if the innate nature of your soul was the God-quality of love, your soul knew only divine Love. She never realized the existence of a relative love that was in opposition to the relative quality of hatred. Your soul thought that God's love was absolute and that there was no other form of love than unconditional love. She did not realize that love could become relative and thereby conditional.

When your soul partook of the forbidden fruit, she suddenly found herself in a relative state of consciousness. In the material octave, love is not absolute: it is a relative quality that has an opposite polarity. In the material octave, love is conditional. Relative love exists on a scale with love at one end and hatred at the other end.

The fall from grace was a shocking and confusing experience for the soul. Your spiritual teacher knew the potential danger and that is why the soul was not supposed to partake of the fruit until it was deemed ready for the initiation. Because the soul partook of the fruit without being ready, she became lost in a relative state of consciousness. How did the soul respond to this new situation?

Before the Fall, the soul would respond to every situation by expressing her God-quality. For example, if the soul's God-quality was love, she would respond to all situations with unconditional love. After the Fall, the soul lost her conscious contact with the spiritual self. The soul's God-quality was anchored in the spiritual self, so the lost soul could no longer comprehend the absolute nature of her God-quality. Therefore, the soul had no other option than to respond to her new situation with the relative version of her God-quality. If the God-quality was love, the soul would now respond with relative, or conditional, love.

This deeply affected the way the soul looked upon herself and her relationship to her spiritual teacher and her spiritual self. In this process of confusion and turmoil, souls tended to go one of two ways. Some souls became polarized towards the negative aspect of their new relative soul-quality. For example, if the soul's God-quality was love, the soul would now respond to the situation with hatred.

The soul felt hatred towards herself for having eaten the forbidden fruit, and the soul projected this relative quality upon the teacher. The soul thought that the teacher would hate her for eating the forbidden fruit, so she accepted the belief that her spiritual teacher was a hateful teacher and that God was a hateful God. The soul reasoned that because of the teacher's hatred, it was necessary and just to hide from the teacher.

Then the soul engaged in a quest to prove that God or the spiritual teacher was wrong from the beginning. Therefore it was never really the soul's fault that she fell; the soul was set up or betrayed by God. In this way, the soul might actually succeed in proving to herself that God was wrong. However, that will not bring the soul back to God.

Some souls became polarized towards the positive aspect of their new relative soul-quality. For example, a soul might become polarized towards relative love. The soul did not want to go back to the teacher because she did not want to admit that she had made a mistake. Therefore, the soul engaged in a quest to prove that she had never made a mistake, and she sought to develop her relative soul-quality. For example, the soul might seek to "perfect" the relative quality of human love. The soul reasoned that by perfecting this relative quality on her own, the spiritual teacher would have to accept the soul.

The soul was attempting to strike a deal with God by thinking that if she could perfect a relative quality, God had to accept the soul as if she had never made a mistake in the first place. Such a soul might master the relative quality; however, doing so would not bring the soul back to God. The soul must look beyond all relativity and give up the idea that she needs to perfect a relative quality. To come back to God, the soul needs to accept her relationship to the spiritual self and begin to express her God-quality.

To come back to God, a soul must step on to the true path of seeking to unite with the spiritual self. To do this, the soul must give up following the false path of trying to prove that God is wrong and the soul is right. It is not a matter of being right or wrong; it is a matter of being who you are.

The ego-quality

The ego was created from the soul's original decision to turn away from God. Therefore the very nature of your ego is determined by the particular quality that your soul used to justify the decision to turn away from God. If your original God-quality was love, then the very nature, or personality, of your ego is hatred, relative love or a combination of both.

Once you begin to understand this, you will have a much better foundation for unmasking your ego. You will be able to understand the particular quality that your ego uses to manipulate your soul. One way to unmask the ego is to examine your default reaction to unexpected situations. For example, some people have a tendency to feel hatred when other people don't do as these people expect.

By understanding the ego's manipulation, it will be easier for you to make a conscious decision not to engage in the particular quality that is the nature of your ego. More importantly, in understanding the negative quality of your ego, you will also come to understand the original God-quality of your soul. You will then be able to consciously cultivate that quality.

If your God-quality was love, then the nature of your ego is hatred or human love. Your ego will seek to make you respond to situations with hatred or with selfish love. To escape your ego, you must make a determined effort to avoid responding to situations or people with these relative qualities. Rather, make an effort to cultivate the quality of divine love so that you can respond to all situations with the purest love of which you are capable. By doing so, you will fortify your soul for the final initiation on the path.

The final initiation requires you to undo the original decision to turn away from God. To undo this decision, you must overcome the illusion that God is a hateful God (or whatever relative quality your soul projected upon God). The key to overcoming this false image of God is to realize that God's love is not conditional; it is unconditional. Because of this unconditional love, your soul never had a reason to turn away from the teacher. Even though you made a mistake by eating the forbidden fruit, your teacher would have accepted you with open arms, and your spiritual teacher is ready to accept you at this very moment. Your teacher's acceptance is unconditional, but to accept the teacher your soul must undo her conditional decision to turn away from the teacher. To this day, that original decision makes your soul feel that she cannot or will not go back to God. The teacher never rejected you; you rejected the teacher. The teacher never ran away from you; you ran away from the teacher. At any moment, you can stop running away, turn around and face your spiritual teacher, who is waiting for you with open arms!

What is your personal God-quality, your God-flame? Your higher self knows the answer to that question. So, by applying the inner approach to knowledge, you can gradually come to understand your original God-quality.

It can be helpful for you to do a bit of soul-searching. Take an objective look at your personality and try to discover your default reaction to unpleasant situations. When something unpleasant or unexpected happens, what are the very first thoughts or feelings that come to you? By understanding your default reaction, you will come to discover the modus operandi of your ego. Once you understand the negative quality that dominates your ego, you can use it to discover the original God-quality of your soul. In this respect, do not forget to use the technique for gaining insights from your higher self (described in part one).

As an example, suppose that when people don't do what you want them to do, your ego responds with hatred or dislike. Your ego might find it difficult to forgive and forget. Your ego-quality is hatred and you think God hates you. In reality, your ego hates God. Part of you might think that you would hate being near God, yet it is only the ego who has this reaction. Your ego also hates your soul, and it wants your soul to feel that you deserve to be hated.

Your God-quality is the opposite, namely love. You must realize that God has always loved you with an unconditional love. However, God has unconditional love for your soul and not for your ego. God does not hate your ego; your ego projects its hatred upon God. God does not hate your ego, because to God the ego simply doesn't exist. If you seek to resolve all feelings of hatred, you can begin to respond to situations with unconditional love. Through unconditional love, you can rise above the ego.

After you discover your ego-quality, you can use the tools given in part one to strip your ego of its power. For example, use a spiritual technique, such as affirmations, to consume the misqualified energy produced through hatred. Then use a technique to uncover and resolve all subconscious computer programs that spring from hatred and cause you to respond with hatred. Seek to uncover all decisions that spring from hatred, and replace them with decisions based on love.

After you discover your God-quality, you can make a conscious effort to overcome all resistance to it. Focus your attention on that quality and visualize how it penetrates every aspect of your being and world. Eventually you can begin to understand and accept the unconditional nature of your God-quality, and you can start to cultivate it. Gradually, you will begin to accept that you are meant to be that God-quality in action on Earth.

God has many obvious qualities, such as love, power, justice, truth, wisdom et cetera. Your soul might be created from one of these general qualities, but your soul also has an individual God-flame. It is this flame that you truly need to discover, and this revelation can only come from your higher self.

The modus operandi of your ego

No matter what God-quality you have, the ego is always using the same strategy in its attempts to imprison your soul. Though people's specific qualities are different, the strategy is the same. Let us look at the key elements of the ego's strategy.

- Because the ego was created from the relative version of your God-quality, it uses this relative quality to manipulate your soul. If the ego is created from hatred, it expresses hatred towards your soul for making mistakes (the ego knows no other way to react).

• The ego projects its relative quality upon God. If the ego is created from the relative version of God love, it thinks that God is hateful or that God's love is conditional.

• The ego is attempting to make your soul accept the ego's relative image of God.

• The ego wants your soul to think that God is using the perverted version of your God-quality, the ego-quality, to judge and condemn you.

• The ego wants your soul to fear going back to God. It seeks to accomplish this by making your soul believe that God will judge you according to the ego-quality.

• The ego wants your soul to continue to hide from God so that you do not experience the pain of God's judgment.

• The ego wants the soul to accept the illusion that the soul has made such a grave mistake (by eating the forbidden fruit or by doing something wrong in the material world) that the soul could never go back to God.

• The ego wants the soul to feel unworthy to face God so that the soul will remain under the ego's control.

• The ego wants the soul to accept the ego as a substitute for the spiritual self, and thereby for God. The ego wants the soul to treat it as a god, as an authority that cannot be gainsaid.

It should be easy to see that the ego fits the mold of a classical tyrant who wants to control you and exercise absolute power over your soul.

As you begin to unmask your ego and rediscover your true divine identity, remember that you should never give power to imperfect manifestations by putting too much attention on them. Jesus admonished people to be "wise as serpents and harmless as doves." This statement contains the key to overcoming the ego.

When you know that the ego exists and understand how it enslaves your soul, you can begin to remove the toxic energies and toxic beliefs that your ego has used to build prison walls around the soul. After you become wise to the serpent of the ego, avoid focusing your attention upon its imperfections because doing so only feeds energy to the ego. Use your wisdom to avoid being ensnared by the ego, and never think that the ego is your true identity. You are not a material, selfish or limited being. In reality, you are a spiritual being, and you must reclaim your true identity by focusing your attention on the perfection of your God-quality. The key to overcoming your ego-quality is to focus on your God-quality.

Imagine that you find yourself locked inside a dark room. You cannot get out (your soul cannot walk away from the ego), so your only option is to remove the darkness. How do you remove darkness? Darkness has no substance, no reality in itself, so you cannot stuff it into garbage bags and throw it out the window. Darkness can only be removed when you understand that it is an absence of light. Therefore, to overcome the unreality of your personal ego, you must focus your conscious attention on the light of your spiritual self.

Find the little switch deep inside your soul that turns on the light of your spiritual self.

How can you put this understanding to work for you? By realizing that your God-flame can be used as a very practical tool for overcoming your limitations. You can use your God-flame to enhance almost any spiritual technique you practice. For example, you can visualize your God-flame enveloping your personal energy field and consuming all imperfect energies within the field. You can also create affirmations that make use of your God-flame. For example:

I AM the flame of God's unconditional love consuming all hatred (or any negative quality) in my entire consciousness, being and world!

I AM God's unconditional love manifest here!

I AM the flame of God's unconditional love!

According to the Bible, God is a consuming fire. A God-flame consumes all unlike itself. Calling forth your personal God-flame is a powerful spiritual technique that can consume negative energy, your ego and your lower self.

You do not need to fear that your God-flame will consume your true identity. Your true identity, meaning your spiritual self and your soul, were made from the energies of your God-flame and they will not be consumed by that flame. Always remember that you have a God-given right to express your God-flame here on Earth. This is a foundational part of your reason for being.

As you begin to shift your sense of identity away from the ego and the lower self, you will begin to understand and accept that in reality you are a God-flame who is temporarily expressing itself through a physical body. You are in the world but you are not of the world, and your true home is in a spiritual octave. Your soul's deepest longing is to return to your home of light.

DISCOURSE 14:
The True Purpose of the Path

The spiritual path has several stages. At the lowest level, a soul is so identified with the material world and the ego that it completely ignores or denies the spiritual side of life. It either thinks that God does not exist or that God is a remote entity which the soul could not possibly know. At this stage, the ego has complete control over the soul and is doing its utmost to prevent the soul from realizing that life has a spiritual side.

At the next stage, the soul has accepted that life has a spiritual side. The soul might see herself as religious and go to church on Sundays. However, the soul may wear religion as an outer garment without understanding the spiritual aspects of religion. The soul thinks that God is "up there" and that she cannot know God directly. So the ego still has a lot of control and will attempt to make the soul cling to one particular religion or doctrine. The ego wants the soul to feel that as long as she belongs to a particular organization and follows all of the rules and doctrines, the soul will automatically be saved.

At this stage, the main goal of the ego is to prevent you from using the inner approach to knowledge. The ego does not want you to think on your own; it wants you to let some outer authority do your thinking for you. Most importantly, the ego does not want you to discover the universal spiritual element behind all religions. The ego wants you to follow the outer path and remain ignorant about the true, inner path.

Universality behind divisions

As the soul matures, she gradually begins to understand and acknowledge that behind all religious divisions can be found a universal and timeless spirituality. Even though the soul is now consciously aware of the path, the ego still finds it relatively easy to control the soul by using the ego-quality. Because the Fall was such a traumatic experience for the soul, the soul feels bruised and vulnerable. Therefore, the soul easily believes that she is unworthy of knowing God or that she has made such severe mistakes that she can never be forgiven.

The ego can maintain its stranglehold on the soul until the soul begins to recognize the ego's existence, goals and methods. When the soul begins to realize that she must put off the old (mortal) human and put on the new (spiritual) identity, the ego faces its first severe challenge. At this point, the ego will roll out the heavy artillery and use every weapon in its arsenal in a last-ditch attempt to maintain control over the soul. For the ego, this battle is literally a matter of life and death, and it will do anything to prevent the soul from breaking through to a higher level of spiritual awareness. However, let not the term "heavy artillery" fool you into thinking that the ego's weapons are easy to detect. On the contrary, the ego's most potent weapons are so subtle that most people never even realize they are under attack.

- To keep the soul in chains, the ego will try to:
- Make the soul focus on negativity, inharmony and imperfection.
- Make a deal with the soul.
- Make you a relatively good person.

As people think, so are they

The ego knows that you are a slave of your attention, because your attention is what directs your creative energies. Whatever your attention dwells upon will be magnified by your creative potential. Your inner and outer circumstances will directly reflect that on which your attention is focused.

If you have read any other self-help books, you are probably aware that many of them stress the importance of maintaining a positive attitude toward life. Unfortunately, they often fail to tell you how to attain this positive state of mind. You can now see that the key to manifesting a truly positive attitude is to free your mind from toxic energies and subconscious computer programs that pull your conscious mind into negative patterns. However, it is also important to make a conscious decision to take your mind off the imperfect conditions that you don't want and focus it firmly on the perfect conditions that you do want. As with any true decision, this choice should be based on right understanding. To explore why it is so important to focus on perfection, we will consider a scientific and a spiritual explanation, beginning with quantum physics.

When a physicist is observing a subatomic event, it is impossible to predict the outcome because a number of potential outcomes exist in what scientists call the "realm of probability." As previously mentioned, this realm might be an octave that is right above the material octave. When the experiment is performed, one of the probabilities is pulled into the material octave as an actual event. The selection of one probability over others is a product of the measurement situation, including the consciousness of the scientist.

Some physicists believe that because all matter is made from subatomic particles, the laws that govern the subatomic realm also affect the level of everyday events. Although this is by no means scientifically proven, consider the following idea. Suppose you are facing a particular situation that requires you to take action. This situation has ten potential outcomes, and before you take action they exist in a realm of probability. When you do take action, one of these outcomes will manifest in your life.

Let us assume that the quality of these ten possibilities is determined by outer circumstances and other people. In other words, in the short run you cannot change the quality of the possibilities. However, the ten possibilities can be put on a scale from the least desirable to the most desirable. What if you could make sure that the most desirable possibility is the one that will manifest in the material octave?

Quantum physics tells us that the consciousness of the scientist can influence a subatomic event. This seems to indicate that your consciousness can influence the events in your life. In other words, if you allow your attention to focus on the negative aspects of a situation, the least desirable possibility is more likely to manifest. If you focus on the positive side, the most desirable possibility is more likely to manifest. So you can see why you should never let your ego manipulate you into accepting a negative state of mind.

A spiritual reason to be positive

Let us now look at the spiritual reason to be positive. We have seen that when God created the universe, God envisioned an image of what to create. God then projected this image upon the basic substance of creation, namely spiritual light, and the light took on the form envisioned. We have also seen that God created you in God's image, meaning that you have the ability to act as a co-creator. You create the same way God does, through your attention. You have a constant stream of spiritual energy that flows from your spiritual self to your soul. This light is like clay and it can take on any form, perfect or imperfect. So it will take on whatever form your attention is focused upon.

Compare this to a movie theater. The lightbulb inside the projector is like the light from your spiritual self. The movie screen is like your outer circumstance in the material octave, and the filmstrip is like your mind. The driving force behind the movie you see on the screen is the white light radiated by the lamp in the projector. However, the white light is not what appears on the screen. As it passes through the filmstrip in the projector, the white light is colored. What you see on the movie screen is determined by the images on the filmstrip. Likewise, what you see on the screen of life is determined by how the light from your spiritual self is colored by the images and beliefs in your mind. If you want to change the images on the screen of life, you must change the images in your mind. It's that simple!

If you focus your attention on imperfection, then you will create imperfect circumstances in your life. If you make a decision to focus on perfection, you will begin to create perfect circumstances. This will not happen overnight, but it will happen. It is not a matter of wishful thinking: it is a matter of spiritual law, and no human being is exempt from that law. You are constantly creating through your attention. The true meaning of Shakespeare's play Hamlet is to illustrate that you can never stop creating. Whether you act or do not act, you are still creating through the power of your attention. However, while you cannot stop creating, you can choose what to create.

Your ego knows this, and therefore it will use many subtle means to manipulate you into focusing on imperfection. It will seek to make you believe that you cannot improve your life or that you are not worthy of receiving something better. It will seek to make you fear the worst rather than believe in the reality of the spiritual law expressed in the saying, "As people think, so they are." Don't let the ego fool you into accepting a negative outlook on life. It is God's good pleasure to give you the kingdom, but God will not do so against your free will. God will let you create whatever you choose to focus your attention upon.

Because this idea is foundational for personal growth, let us tie it into the concepts described in part one. What gives you the ability to create is a stream of spiritual energy from your I AM Presence. This energy flows into your soul and you express it through your mind. What directs your creative energy is your conscious mind and your attention. However, before the energy reaches the conscious mind, it must pass through your subconscious mind. In your subconscious mind, the spiritual energy passes through a filter made from your subconscious computer programs and the beliefs about yourself and life that give you a sense of identity. As the pure spiritual energy passes through this subconscious filter, its vibration will be changed according to the quality of the filter. It is much like sunlight passing through a stained glass window and taking on the colors of the glass. So your conscious mind is not working with pure energy and this limits your ability to manifest perfection in your life. That is why it is so important for you to start clearing out the toxic energies, subconscious computer programs and toxic beliefs that distort the pure energies of your higher self. As you begin to clean the filter, your conscious mind can make use of more pure and abundant spiritual energy, and this will greatly expand your creative abilities.

Does the ego have a deal for you!

As the ego sees the handwriting on the wall, it will attempt to strike a deal with your soul. The ego will attempt to make your soul believe that if only you will allow it to keep one last thing, one last possession, then it will let go of everything else. In other words, your ego will try to make your soul believe that if you will ignore the original decision to turn away from God, then the ego will surrender everything else, including the lower self.

For many people this can be a tempting proposition. The soul might find such a deal tempting for two reasons:

- The ego has been a part of the soul's sense of identity for so long that the soul may fear letting go of the original decision that created the ego. The soul might fear that she will be alone and incomplete.

- The soul might be reluctant to admit that she made a mistake in her original decision to turn away from God. This reluctance often springs from either fear or pride (or a combination of the two).

Unfortunately, many sincere seekers fall for the temptation to strike a deal with the ego. People who walk the spiritual path are generally open-minded, but some have one particular issue that they either cannot or will not recognize as a problem. This often manifest as a specific belief or belief system or as a peculiar character trait. It is behind such a blind spot that the ego will try to hide. If you refuse to look at your blind spot, your ego can hide for a very long time.

Even people with great attainment on the path can become extremely attached to one point which they do not want to change. It is a spiritual holy cow which the soul considers to be untouchable. Usually, the ego has conjured up some kind of excuse for why the soul does not have to confront this one problem, and the soul has accepted this excuse. The soul might realize that overcoming the ego is a requirement for spiritual growth, so it might be willing to look at any other aspect of the lower self and the ego as long as no one

The True Purpose of the Path

attempts to force the soul to kill the holy cow. If someone attempts to make the soul confront this hang-up, the soul will respond with hostility. If you find yourself responding to a certain idea with an unusual hostility, your ego is hiding behind the belief that is challenged by that idea. Be on the lookout for this reaction, and use it to unmask your ego!

If you were to look behind the surface of this blind spot, you would realize that it is hiding the original decision that caused the soul to turn away from God. The soul has become so attached to this decision that the decision has become an integral part of her sense of identity. The soul is not willing to take an objective look at the situation and recognize that it is this very decision that stands between the soul and her reunion with the spiritual self.

In reality, the entire conglomerate of the lower self is made from variations of this original decision. Obviously, if the ego were to successfully convince the soul to accept the bargain to leave the original decision untouched, then the soul would have no chance of walking all the way home. In reality, a soul can make great strides and great progress on the spiritual path, only to be stopped in her tracks at the very doorstep to eternal life. Right as the soul is ready and prepared to take the final step, that original decision comes back to haunt her and to abort her progress on the path. Don't let this happen to you!

Many people have pursued the spiritual path with great diligence and they have made great progress in healing their psychological wounds. Yet in the very end, they have failed to take the final step. These people often put themselves into a state of consciousness in which they believe that they are very spiritually advanced, and they often look at themselves as having great attainment. In one sense, they have made great strides and they do have great attainment. Yet if they do not take the final step, then all of their other attainment comes to naught.

Some souls believe they have made such great sacrifices on the path that they do not have to surrender that one last thing. They believe they have sacrificed enough on the altar of spiritual progress. However, to become acceptable, the offering must include all aspects of the ego. In fact, were a soul to undo the original decision to forsake her spiritual teacher, then all else would immediately be forgiven. If the soul does not undo the original decision, then all of her progress will fall short of the mark.

This somber fact does not mean that God is unreasonable or unfair. It was the soul who made the original decision that caused her to fall into a lower state of consciousness. Therefore, to ascend back into a spiritual state of consciousness, it is the soul who needs to undo that decision.

A relatively good person

Let us now consider another ace that your ego has up its sleeve. As you begin to recognize your ego-quality, you need to remember that it is not the opposite of your God-quality. Your God-quality has no opposition. Your ego was created from the relative version of your God-quality. This relative quality has two opposite polarities, such as love and hatred. While it is easy to see that hatred is different from divine love, it is important to realize that human, or relative, love is also different from divine love. If you do not make this distinction, your ego will use it against you.

As you begin to diminish the negative aspects of your ego-quality, you will naturally begin to cultivate the positive aspects of that quality. For example, you might begin to diminish the negative pull of human hatred and cultivate the positive quality of human love. Throughout the ages, many

The True Purpose of the Path

people have made great efforts to cultivate a positive quality, such as love. This is a perfectly valid approach, but it is only valid at a certain level on the path.

Cultivating human love is an important step in the growth of your soul; however, you must never stop there. The goal of the path is to free your soul from all attachment to the relativity of the ego and the material world. Therefore, your soul must rise above all relative love and embody the absolute, unconditional love of God.

Unfortunately, some people fail to recognize the need to rise above relativity. They make a great and sincere effort to free themselves from hatred and to cultivate love, and then they begin to feel that they have "made it." This can lead to a subtle feeling that because they have cultivated human love to such a high degree, God simply has to save them. These people think they have made a deal with God. This illusion can be greatly magnified if other people who are also caught in a relative state of consciousness begin to recognize a person as being good or spiritual.

The ego will immediately exploit this opportunity to make the soul feel pride over having cultivated a relative human quality. The ego's motto can be expressed by the saying, "If you can't beat them, join them." If the ego cannot make you feel unworthy, it will attempt to make you feel superior and thereby cause you to fall into the trap of pride. If you study the lives of truly spiritual persons, such as Mahatma Gandhi, Padre Pio and Mother Theresa, you will see that they all had great humility. Then contrast the lives of these people to some of the so-called great leaders of the world who were motivated by pride and a quest for power.

At the lower levels of the path your ego will use the weapon of unworthiness, and at the higher levels of the path your ego will use the weapon of pride. The key to overcoming this strategy is to realize that only your God-quality is the acceptable offering. Whatever your ego-quality is, you must rise above it.

Cultivating human love can help you advance on the path, but it can never take you all the way home. If it causes you to fall into the trap of pride, it will take you in the opposite direction. The way out is to reach for your higher self and allow it to help you see beyond all relativity. If you are aware of the trap of unworthiness and pride and if you reach for your God-quality, you truly can rise above all of the temptations and illusions of your ego.

The spiritual staircase

After all this talk about overcoming the ego, it might seem that the most important element of the path is to escape the downward pull of the ego. One might think that when a soul has risen above the ego, the soul is home free. In reality, the ego is not the major hurdle for the soul to overcome. The most important part of the path is for the soul to overcome the false sense of identity that she created after losing conscious contact with the spiritual self. The soul must overcome the pseudo identity that makes her think she is a material, limited, mortal being who is separated from God.

One might compare the spiritual path to a spiral staircase. As you climb towards the top of the staircase, you must face a very important choice. This test requires you to overcome the final, and in a sense, the only obstacle to your spiritual progress. This obstacle is the original decision that caused your soul to turn away from the spiritual teacher, symbolized by the God of the Garden of Eden. The very last initiation requires you to come to a full recognition of that decision. Then you must consciously choose to undo that decision by replacing it with a right decision. You must choose life, not death. You must choose your spiritual self over the ego.

The True Purpose of the Path

You are on your own

As already mentioned, there are spiritual beings, such as your higher self and the saints and sages of the ages, who are willing to assist you on your spiritual path. Yet they cannot do everything for you. No spiritual teacher will ever violate your free will or make decisions for you. Therefore, no spiritual teacher, including your higher self and your spiritual self, could possibly undo your soul's original decision to turn away from God. That decision was made by the soul, and it was made by the soul alone. So it must be undone by the soul alone.

You can receive great inspiration by considering the final moments of Jesus as he was hanging on the cross. Those who nailed him to the cross were completely identified with their egos. Jesus represents the soul who is nailed to the cross by the ego and by the forces of this world. Jesus could not take himself down from the cross of wood, and your soul cannot take herself down from the cross of separation from God. How can your soul escape the cross of her pseudo identity? The only force that can set the soul free from the cross is the spiritual self. However, this can only happen when the soul surrenders herself completely to the spiritual self.

The soul was created as an extension of the spiritual self, and originally the soul formed a perfect polarity with the spiritual self. The soul was the yin, or passive, element in this polarity, and the spiritual self was the yang, or active, element. Before the Fall the soul fully realized that she could act only because she was using the energy of the spiritual self. The soul also knew that by following the directions of the spiritual self, she would always be in accordance with the laws of God and therefore she would not misqualify energy. The soul realized the truth in Jesus' statement, "I of my own self (the soul) can do nothing; it is the Father (the spiritual self) within me who does the work." Therefore the soul allowed the spiritual self to be the doer in her life.

When the soul lost conscious contact with the spiritual self, she began to believe that she could act on her own. When a soul is separated from the spiritual self, she no longer realizes that she can only act by using God's energy. Therefore she builds a false sense of identity as a material being who is acting by using the energies of the material world. When the soul acts without conscious contact with the spiritual self, she misqualifies the pure energies of God. Thereby the soul binds herself to a cross that is made from material energy.

Before the soul can take the final step on the path, she must choose to let go of the illusion that she can do anything without the spiritual self. She must let go of the illusion that she is separated from the spiritual self and that she has a life of her own. This is a decision that the soul needs to make without any help from the spiritual self or her spiritual teachers, and it can be a difficult decision.

The final illusion

The ego will seek to ensnare the soul by using many deceptive ideas. However, the most deceptive of all is the illusion that the soul is separated from the spiritual self. This illusion was not created by the ego, because the ego was created after the soul chose to hide from her spiritual teacher and thereby separate herself from God. The illusion was created by the soul after she realized she had fallen into a relative state of consciousness.

When a soul becomes aware of the spiritual path, she must make a conscious choice to engage in that path. As the soul climbs the path, she must make a sincere effort to overcome the illusions of the ego and the downward pull of material energies. When a soul has made many sincere efforts

The True Purpose of the Path

and has achieved considerable success on the path, the soul might feel that she has done so by her own efforts. Unfortunately, this is a subtle and dangerous illusion that springs from the soul's sense of separation from God.

Your soul cannot save herself. Imagine that you are wearing a pair of old-fashioned leather boots. Each boot has a leather strap that you can use to pull the boot onto your foot. Now imagine that you put a finger through each bootstrap and try to lift your body off the floor by pulling on the straps. If you know about the law of action and reaction, you will realize that this is an impossible task. To generate the force used to pull on the straps, you must push your feet against the floor. Therefore, the downward push of your feet cancels out the upward pull of your arms and you get nowhere. Thus the old saying that you cannot pull yourself up by your bootstraps.

Likewise, the soul cannot escape the downward pull of the material world by using the energies of the material world. This explains the saying that without God's grace, without God's spiritual energy, no flesh (no fallen souls) would be saved. The soul can walk the spiritual path only by reaching beyond the material world.

In order to make spiritual progress, the soul must free herself from the downward pull of material energy. She can do so only by invoking high-frequency spiritual energy. That energy cannot be produced by the soul; it must come through the higher self. The soul also needs to learn to make right choices. Because the soul is in a lower state of consciousness, she has no direct knowledge of the laws of God. She can know these laws only through the higher self.

The conclusion is that the soul cannot save herself. In fact, once the soul has fallen into a lower state of consciousness, she cannot understand the spiritual path or even recognize the need for salvation. The soul would remain in this state of spiritual blindness unless some outer force was sent into this world to enlighten her. Unless God sent his emissaries into the material world, no soul would ever discover the path. Unless God's emissaries helped the soul, the soul would not be able to take a single step on the path.

The inner savior of your soul is the higher self, which acts as an emissary between your soul and your spiritual self. However, God has also sent outer saviors in the form of spiritual teachers, such as Jesus, Buddha, Krishna and many others.

The all-important conclusion is that the spiritual path is very different from any other activity in the material world because it is not an activity through which the soul acts on her own. The soul can make spiritual progress only by acting as part of a team composed of the soul, the higher self and one or more spiritual teachers. The soul must make a sincere effort, but she is only successful when she uses the energies of the spiritual self and follows the understanding she receives from the higher self. As Jesus said, "My Father (the spiritual self) works hitherto, and I (the soul) work." If the soul does not overcome the illusion that she can act on her own, she cannot pass the final initiation on the path.

The final initiation

Only a higher spiritual force, or rather the spiritual self, can take the soul down from the cross of materialism. However, before the savior of the soul can do anything, the soul needs to surrender herself completely to God. The soul must surrender her sense of being separated from God and the illusion that she can do anything without the spiritual self. The soul's sense of separation, her false identity, must die, just as the body of Jesus died on the cross. That act of surrender must be made by the soul without outside assistance.

When you consider the ministry of Jesus, it becomes obvious that he had total faith in God's willingness to assist him, and he made many statements to this effect. Jesus was also accustomed to having conscious contact with his higher self and with spiritual beings in higher octaves, as recorded in the description of his transfiguration. Yet at the hour of greatest need, at the hour of greatest turmoil, a very peculiar thing happened. As Jesus was hanging helpless on the cross, he suddenly cried out, "My God, my God, why have you forsaken me?"

This question illustrates the final requirement on the path, namely for the soul to let go of her sense of separation from God, her sense that she has an identity apart from the spiritual self. The soul must give up her mortal sense of identity. When you come to the final decision on the spiritual path, your higher self and your spiritual teachers must withdraw from you. For the soul this can be a shocking experience. As stated earlier, the soul was not created to be alone but to be in a polarity with the spiritual self. When the soul lost contact with the spiritual self, she created the ego, and the ego became a surrogate for the spiritual self. As the soul walks the path, she gradually overcomes her codependence on the ego. However, the soul does so by coming to rely upon the higher self and her spiritual teachers.

Therefore, the soul gradually becomes accustomed to always having support and protection from spiritual beings and from the higher self. The soul is thinking that she is making great progress on the path and that she is almost home free. Just when the soul thinks she has reached the final moment of triumph, she is faced with her most difficult task. She is thrown into what can be called "the dark night of the soul."

At this very moment, the spiritual teachers of the soul must withdraw. The soul is crucified by the ego, and while hanging on the cross the soul feels that God has forsaken her.

In reality, God never forsakes the soul, but God must respect the free will of the soul. Therefore, God must allow the soul to make the final decision on her own.

A matter of surrender

The ministry of Jesus was meant to demonstrate the initiations that a soul must face on the spiritual path, as illustrated by the events of his life, including the fourteen stations of the cross. Obviously, every human being does not have to be nailed to a wooden cross, but every person is nailed to a cross of misqualified energy.

Consider what happens to Jesus after he cries out to God. Jesus is in great agony, and this symbolizes how difficult it can be for the soul to let go of her sense of identity as a mortal being who is separated from God. Then a great peace comes over Jesus and he "gives up the ghost." This symbolizes that the soul has finally made peace with God and given up the ghostly identity as a mortal being.

If you did not know that this final initiation was coming, your soul would be profoundly shocked. When you are aware of this final initiation on the path, you can prepare yourself for it. Jesus was willing to provide a graphic illustration of the spiritual path. By learning from his example, you can prepare yourself for the initiation so that you do not experience it as a shock. Instead of being unprepared, you can gradually let go of your mortal identity and accept your immortal identity.

To prepare yourself for the final initiation, you can:

- Understand why your soul made the original decision to turn away from God. Once you understand the nature of that decision, and the motives that prompted the soul to make that decision, it becomes much easier to face the initiation of the dark night of the soul.

The True Purpose of the Path

- Realize and accept that your soul cannot act on her own and that she cannot save herself. Your soul became caught in the material world because she tried to act on her own, and as long as she continues to do so, she will only sink deeper into materialism. Therefore your soul needs to surrender herself to the loving guidance of the higher self. In fact, one might say that the vital element of the spiritual path is an act, or many acts, of surrender.

- Understand, acknowledge and accept that you are not separated from God and you never were separated from God. Make the conscious choice to surrender this subtle and pervasive illusion.

The final surrender

The utmost purpose of the spiritual path is to prepare your soul for the final initiation whereby she can win her eternal victory as a God-free spiritual being. For this to happen, your ego and your soul's sense of human, or mortal, identity must die. Consequently, the path can be seen as a process whereby the soul gradually comes to the point where she is willing to let go of her limited sense of identity. The soul, who created the ego and the mortal identity, must be willing to let her own creation die. The soul must be willing to lose this imperfect and mortal life.

However, the soul cannot exist in a vacuum. Therefore, the soul cannot let go of the ego until she has something that can replace the ego, and that something is the spiritual self. But before the soul can accept the spiritual self, she must:

- Overcome the false image of God. The soul must overcome the image of a God that is characterized by the soul's ego-qualities. Instead, the soul must accept that God is a being who has only absolute God-qualities and that these God-qualities are expressed unconditionally.

- Overcome the illusion that the soul can act without God's energies.

- Overcome the illusion that the soul is separated from God, and understand and accept that it never was and never could be separated from God.

God created the entire world of form out of God's own substance. Without God, nothing was made. Therefore, God is all and in all. If God is omnipresent, how can there be any place where God is not? And if there is no place where God is not found, how could the soul ever be separated from God? Therefore, the sense of separation can only be an illusion and it can only exist as long as the soul, through her free will, accepts the illusion.

The path is a process whereby the soul puts off the old self-image and puts on the new self-image. The soul loses a false sense of identity only to win a true sense of identity. Consider Jesus' statement, "He who loses his life for my sake shall find it." This statement is a divine promise. The promise is that when you are willing to lose your sense of identity as a mortal being, you will find a new sense of identity as an immortal spiritual being. This is not a matter of becoming a spiritual being but of realizing that you are and always were a spiritual being.

Overcoming the dark night of the soul

Why does a soul have to go through the initiation called the dark night of the soul? Because there is no other way the soul can come to realize and accept her true identity.

The True Purpose of the Path

The soul was originally created by God. She was created from God's light, and she was created in God's image. After the Fall, the soul lost her true sense of identity, but she could never lose her potential to regain that identity. Because the soul carries within her the seed of her divine identity, the soul has the potential to self-realize and to become the spiritual being that she truly is. The real goal of the spiritual path is to raise the soul to her true identity. To reclaim that identity, the soul must overcome the illusion that she is incomplete. The soul must realize that to become whole she doesn't need anything from outside herself.

At the lower stages of the path, the soul cannot pull herself up by her bootstraps. She needs help from an outer savior, and she needs the understanding of a spiritual teaching. As the soul climbs the path, she must begin to overcome the illusion that she is incomplete. The soul must realize that she has everything she needs within herself, or rather within the spiritual self.

As the soul first steps onto the spiritual path and recognizes the spiritual side of life, she naturally thinks of God as something or someone outside herself. The soul tends to think that God is somewhere "out there." As the soul matures on the path, she must overcome this illusion. She must realize the truth behind the statements made by Jesus, "The Kingdom of God is within you!" and "Ye are gods." The soul must realize and accept that she is not separated from God and that she is not different from God.

You begin by overcoming the illusion that you are separated from God. However, once you realize that you are not separated from God, you must draw the only logical conclusion. You are not separated from God because you are God—you are God individualized.

Unfortunately, the present religious climate on planet Earth makes it difficult for people to accept this fact. However, as you overcome the ego, you will also overcome the belief that accepting your God-identity is some sort of blasphemy. If you apply the inner approach to knowledge, you will come to accept that this is not blasphemy but supreme realism. If you can accept the statement that you are God individualized, then you need not experience the dark night of the soul. Instead, you can put off the last part of the old man and put on the totality of the God-man, or God-woman.

Consider carefully why God sent Jesus to the Earth. Did God send Jesus to show all people how wonderful God's only son is so that everyone else could feel unworthy to inherit the Kingdom of God? Does it really make sense that God would send Jesus to make everyone else feel like sinners? Or did God send Jesus to be an example that all others can follow? Consider the statements, "The works that I do, you shall do also" and "Let that mind be in you which was also in Christ Jesus!"

If you apply the inner approach to knowledge, you will realize that Jesus came to outline and exemplify a spiritual path that all souls have the potential to follow, and so did all other spiritual leaders. Accepting that Jesus is an example to follow is not blasphemy. By accepting this you do not degrade or take away from the mission of Jesus. In reality, your acceptance of Jesus as an exemplar is the only way that the true mission of Jesus can be fulfilled. Do you really believe that Jesus wants you to misunderstand or ignore his true mission? Or do you believe that he wants to draw all men and women unto himself? Do you think he can draw you unto him against your free will?

The choice is yours: To be who you are in God or not to be who you are—that is the question. Choose to be who you are as a spiritual God-free being!

-compliance